# HOME
# WISDOM

The Old Farmer's Almanac Home Library

# HOME WISDOM

*A Commonsense*

*Guide to Solving*

*Everyday Problems*

## Jon Vara

AND THE EDITORS OF
*The Old Farmer's Almanac*

OLD FARMER'S ALMANAC HOME LIBRARY
Series Editor: Sarah Elder Hale
Consulting Editor: Susan Peery
Copy Editor: Barbara Jatkola
Art Director: Karen Savary
Cover Illustration: Sara Love
Illustrations, pp. 14-15, 34-35, 55, 74-75, 94-95, 115, 134-135: Jim Carson

LIBRARY OF CONGRESS CATALOGING-IN-PUBLICATION DATA
Home wisdom : a commonsense guide to solving everyday problems /
Jon Vara and the editors of The Old farmer's almanac.
p. cm. — (The Old farmer's almanac home library)
Includes bibliographical references and index.
ISBN 0-7835-4937-7
1. Home economics.  I. Vara, Jon.   II: Old farmer's almanac.
III. Series.
TX158.H664   1997
640 — dc21   97-8172 CIP

Distributed in the book trade by Time-Life Books, Inc.

TIME-LIFE BOOKS IS A DIVISION OF TIME LIFE INC.

TIME-LIFE CUSTOM PUBLISHING
Vice President and Publisher: Terry Newell
Associate Publisher: Teresa Hartnett
Vice President of Sales and Marketing: Neil Levin
Director of New Product Development: Quentin McAndrew
Director of Special Sales: Liz Ziehl
Director of Editorial Development: Jennifer Pearce

TIME-LIFE is a trademark of Time Warner Inc. U.S.A.

# Contents

# Foreword

OR MORE THAN 205 YEARS, *THE OLD FARMER'S ALMANAC* has been written to be read on a daily basis in short snatches of time. From my perusal of the early editions, I have concluded that these daily offerings of wisdom — whether about the home, cooking, gardening, or just plain living — were far shorter and more concise than in recent years, and I think I know why.

The explanation stems from the fact that because the Almanac was referred to every day throughout the year, it was usually hung on a nail with a long piece of string. (These days, we provide a hole in the Almanac for that very purpose.) And where do you suppose most people hung it? Let's just say it was a place visited regularly by everyone in the household and where a little reading could be helpful in many ways.

Now take into account that the early Almanac editors realized that during the cold winter months — or, for that matter, during the balmy mosquito season — they would need to inform and entertain their readers quickly, much like television producers think today. "Burn or sweep your chimneys," advised the 1793 edition for January 31 of that year. That was a quick, snappy, useful reminder — the 18th-century version of a sound bite. For February 9, 1793, the equally concise advice was "Get your tools in order for spring work."

With the advent of indoor plumbing in the 20th century, the Almanac's editorial fare became more relaxed. Many people continued to hang the Almanac from a nail in the bathroom, but it was now edited to be read in more generous segments of time. The early nuggets of wisdom became full-length features on everything from good dining room table conversation to how to build a sturdy picnic table.

We still strive to include a few short, snappy pieces of home wisdom in each issue — the sort of information suitable for reading in a cold, drafty little house located just beyond the woodpile. "Take out a six-month loan in the fall," the Almanac advised recently, "and the winter will fly by like nothing." Now those few words are worth a book.

## What Is *The Old Farmer's Almanac?*

First of all, it's the oldest continuously published periodical in North America. It was established in 1792 by Robert B. Thomas, a Massachusetts schoolteacher whose name still appears on the familiar yellow cover, and it has appeared annually on the American scene every year since.

Like any publication legitimately calling itself an almanac, it is also, as such books were known in ancient times, a "calendar of the heavens." In other words, one of its primary duties is to provide the astronomical structure of the coming year on a daily basis.

Perhaps what *The Old Farmer's Almanac* is most of all, however, is a vast compendium of useful and entertaining information. Its major subjects include food, gardening, home remedies, history, and odd facts that you just won't find anywhere else. Oh, yes, it has weather forecasts, too. We can't forget those.

In the past decade, during which the circulation has skyrocketed to include some 9 million readers annually, the Almanac has added a feature section covering current consumer tastes and trends — from collectibles to fashions to health news to money-saving ideas to, well, just about everything going on in America today.

So even though the Almanac is old, it is also brand-new every year. And in addition to being America's oldest publication, perhaps it has become, over these many years, America's most loved publication as well.

JUDSON D. HALE, SR.
Editor-in-Chief
*The Old Farmer's Almanac*
(The 12th editor since 1792)

# Introduction

IDEALLY, A PERSON'S HOME SHOULD BE A COMFORTABLE, secure refuge from the turmoil and confusion of the wider world. It's the place where you can throw another log on the fire — or, if you prefer, slip a rented movie into the VCR — and lose yourself in its warm, flickering glow, wrapped in a sense of utter peace and contentment.

It's a fine, romantic image, and one that is not entirely at odds with reality. For most of us, though, that blissful state is no more than an occasional treat, if only because we spend much of our time away from home and can't help bringing outside problems and concerns in the door with us when we return. And most houses — no, make that all houses — generate a steady stream of problems and concerns on their own.

This is not especially evident to those who don't own a home. To the nonhomeowner, houses are on the same level as rocks and trees. They're everywhere you look, just standing there year after year with no apparent help from anyone. How much help could something so big and permanent really need?

The answer, of course, is plenty. In addition to the routine housekeeping chores such as vacuuming, dusting, scrubbing, and straightening, there are at least three major categories of long-term projects. The first includes regular seasonal tasks: taking down the screens and putting up the storm windows; cleaning autumn leaves out of the gutters and downspouts.

Then there are the larger projects that draw steadily nearer for years until they can no longer be ignored. Scraping and painting the siding comes to mind here, or tearing off and replacing the roof.

And finally, just to keep things interesting, your home life will be punctuated by random disaster from time to time. Your septic tank will back up into the cellar. A family of skunks will take up residence in your chimney. Two hours after you take off on a three-week vacation, your freezer will take a deep shuddering breath and die, leaving you with 200 pounds of hideously spoiled food to deal with when you return.

To handle such problems successfully, you need to know something about your home and how it works. But the key word here is something.

You don't, for example, need to know much about roofing to tear off and replace a roof. You don't necessarily need tools, a ladder, or the right kind of nails. At a minimum, you need only to know that (a) all roofs eventually leak and need to be replaced and (b) when a roof does begin to leak, it's time to put a saucepan under the drip and call a good roofing contractor.

Any knowledge beyond that is optional. You may decide to monitor the condition of your roof from time to time by standing across the street and peering up at it with binoculars. You can read up on roofing techniques (you'll find a surprising number of books on the subject at your local library). When you decide the time is ripe, you may even decide to climb up on the roof and tackle the job yourself.

If you're the sort of person who enjoys such things, you'll probably find doing all that deeply satisfying. And if you're not — if you're the saucepan-and-phone-call type — you'll be deeply satisfied not to have to. As the proverb says, there are more ways to the woods than one.

When it comes to enjoying a happy home life, what you know about yourself is at least as important as what you know about your home. In reading this book — or any other book that presumes to offer suggestions for managing your affairs — you should feel free to take some of what is offered as informative and possibly useful, while regarding other things with skepticism, if not actual hoots of derision.

Even between crises, you'll learn, your home is a remarkable place. Pull up a chair, throw a log on the fire, and enjoy. Does anyone hear water dripping?

# *Chapter 1*

# The Clutter Conundrum,

## or Establishing an Efficient Level of Disorganization

*There seems to be a kind of order in the universe, in the movement of the stars and the turning of the earth and the changing of the seasons, and even in the cycle of human life. But human life itself is almost pure chaos.*

— *KATHERINE ANNE PORTER (1890–1980)*

LMOST EVERYONE HAS A JUNK DRAWER. TRADITIONALLY found in the kitchen, it's a sort of organizational safety net, a haven for things that would otherwise have nowhere to go: hand tools too badly worn or damaged to use but too good to throw away; unidentifiable but possibly important hardware items; rolls of tape and coils of wire; single partly used tubes of two-part epoxy glue; hose clamps and miscellaneous springs; quarts of mixed nuts, bolts, nails, and screws.

In addition to such useful — or at least potentially useful — items, most junk drawers also contain a sprinkling of forlorn objects that wound up there for no good reason and stayed because there has never been any good reason to remove them. Among other things, my junk drawer contains a scattering of pennies, two fluorescent orange golf balls (no one in my family plays golf), a disposable wooden ice cream spoon, several small nondescript stones, a broken clamshell, and a grimy, battered candle.

Although junk drawers play an important part in the management of most households, they're seldom mentioned in polite society. We're careful to leave them closed when we have company. Home-improvement authorities pretend they don't exist. Even homeowners who have no qualms about discussing their septic-tank problems at the dinner table seem to draw the line at bringing up the junk drawer.

Why? It's an embarrassment. No one likes to seem disorganized, and to admit that you have a junk drawer is to admit that there's a part of your house where disorganization is officially given free rein. We know it's there, and we may even suspect that others have one, too, but we still don't like to talk about it.

That's a shame, because if we *did* talk about our junk drawers, most of us would quickly realize that we're no more disorganized than the next person. The plain truth is that hardly anyone is naturally organized. From a biological perspective, organizing things is about the most unnatural human activity imaginable.

After all, in the good old hunting-and-gathering days (for the vast majority of human history), there was nothing to organize. Everything we needed was scattered around outside, and we had only to go out and get it.

That wasn't necessarily easy — it involved a lot of running and climbing and jumping and digging, not to mention occasional close-quarters combat with giant cave bears — but at least we didn't have to go to the trouble of dividing things into categories and deciding where to put them. Nature had already taken care of that: fish lived in the water, eggs were found in bird's nests, fruits and berries grew on trees and bushes, and roots grew under the ground.

Not surprisingly, evolution tended to favor those with the ability to recognize and work with such naturally existing systems. The occasional oddball who showed an interest in developing new concepts of organization — maybe by hanging around the cave and sorting the digging sticks by length while the rest of the clan was out hunting mammoths — probably had a very difficult time finding a mate.

Things went on like this for a million years or so. But somewhere around 5,000 years ago — practically the other day in evolutionary terms — we stumbled upon agriculture, and life suddenly got a lot more complicated.

Now we needed hoes and spades and plows. We needed to figure out how much of each year's crop to save for next year's seed, how much ground to prepare for planting in the spring, and how to manage and distribute surplus crops. This led to the development of counting and writing and to a steady increase in the human population.

Soon there were so many of us that things started getting crowded and chaotic. We had so much to keep track of that we had to split up into more or less specialized groups — national governments, advertising agencies, Cub Scout troops, health maintenance organizations. That brings us to the present, where a relative handful of people who are naturally good at organizing things — those guys who used to be in charge of the digging sticks — have turned the tables on the rest of us and are now pretty much running the show. The story of organization, in short, is the story of civilization.

That's why a cluttered junk drawer seems so, well, primitive. Like our ancestral environment, it's a self-sustaining natural system over which we have little control — a tangible reminder of the hunter-gatherer that lurks in all of us. At some unconscious level, the suburban homeowner pawing through the junk drawer for a pop rivet — instinctively zeroing in on the back portion of the drawer, where natural sifting and settling causes the smaller items to congregate — probably imagines that he is hunched over a rotting log, searching for edible grubs.

Admittedly, all of that is more or less academic. Unless you're prepared to leave everything behind and head off to the forests of the Pacific Northwest to live with Bigfoot — a solution that poses some major problems of its own — you'll have to come to terms with the need for organization.

*At some unconscious level, the suburban homeowner pawing through the junk drawer for a pop rivet probably imagines that he is hunched over a rotting log, searching for edible grubs.*

At this point, it might be nice to rattle off some useful and comforting rules — something along the lines of "The 23 Golden Rules of Organizing Your Life." But that particular wheel was invented long ago and has been reinvented many times since. If a proven, solid, workable plan is what you're after, head for the self-help section of the bookstore and take your pick from among the upbeat step-by-step books about organizing your home or business or family or love life. There are plenty to choose from. There are so many, in fact, that you have to wonder why there are still so many disorganized people. In short, can good intentions and an $18 book really turn your life around?

OK, that was a rhetorical question. But things are not hopeless. The real secret of successful organizing comes down to one deceptively simple concept: *do the minimum*. A good system of organization, like a good government, must strike a balance between anarchy on the one hand and tyranny on the other. And if you're not sure where that balance lies, it's far better to err on the side of excess freedom, if only because too much organization has a way of creating a backlash that leaves you less organized than ever.

For example, consider one common organizing device — the wall-mounted sheet of Peg-Board or plywood, with the outlines of various tools marked in paint to show where each should hang. It's a simple, straightforward system that has probably been used for centuries. It's easy to set up and absolutely logical. And because it flies in the face of human nature, it almost never works.

The basic problem with the tool board is that it's too fussy to put up with for long. When you go out to the garage to put away the hammer, the painted outline tells you not only *where* to hang it but precisely *how* — with the head facing right and the claws facing left. Although this is pointless, the tool board insists that it's not. You may play along with it for a while, but unless you have an unusually high threshold for petty annoyance, you'll eventually rebel. You'll start hanging the hammer backward deliberately, out of spite. Soon you'll take to leaving it on the workbench. In the end, it'll probably end up back in the kitchen junk drawer.

*If you never misplace anything, you're already too organized. Let your life get a little messier.*

Although disorganization is ordinarily thought of as inefficient, inefficiency can result from too much organization. The goal, once again, is a happy medium. You should expect to spend a few minutes occasionally wandering around the house, looking for things you have misplaced. If you never misplace anything, you're already too organized. Let your life get a little messier. Any time you lose as a result will be more than offset by savings elsewhere — in less time spent keeping things picked up and put away.

When you come right down to it, disorganization is really just one more organizational technique. Accept that, and you're well on your way to making your peace with the junk drawer. And why shouldn't you? You're only human.

*Had I been present at the creation, I would have given some useful hints for the better ordering of the universe.* — ALPHONSO THE LEARNED (1221–1284)

# Paper Clutter
*BY MAUDE SALINGER*

Picture this scene: You're rummaging through a pile of paper stacked on top of the kitchen counter (since you long ago ran out of room to store stuff on your desk), searching in vain for those theater tickets you need tonight. Do you find the tickets? No. But you do find six months' worth of bank statements neatly wrapped with a rubber band, last week's mail, all those recipes you've clipped and been meaning to try, catalogs (same company, different seasons), school notices, bills (there's that credit card statement you thought you'd lost!), newspapers, magazines (there might be an important article you'll want to save), receipts, notes, and "to do" lists. Why does all this stuff seem to accumulate faster than you can read it, file it, pay it, give it away, or throw it out?

If clutter is the bane of your existence, take heart — you're not alone. Getting rid of clutter may take some time and effort, but there is hope. Here are the basic principles, straight from the experts.

## Clutter Busting: Two Simple Steps

The problem of clutter can be broken down into two simple elements: (1) too much stuff; (2) no place to put it.

The solution to number one (reducing the stuff) helps, but until — and unless — you set up a system for organizing the stuff, you'll be right back where you began, shuffling through those mounds of paper. So let's begin with number two.

**Problem:** No place to put it.
**Solution:** Use a file cabinet.

Most of us spend at least as much time handling paper as we do preparing food. We wouldn't think of going without a kitchen, so why pretend we don't need a desk? Set up a permanent work center — in the bedroom, kitchen, or den — that will be available to you at all times. If you absolutely don't have room for a desk, use the dining room table. But *do* get a file cabinet. Buy one with built-in metal frames for hanging file folders, or purchase add-on frames for each drawer. Also, get a supply of hanging folders.

## Set Up a Filing System

First, gather up everything you want to store in your file cabinet. Then begin sorting it into stacks or general categories such as bills, instruction booklets, correspondence, school records, and so forth. Each stack will become a separate file, so pay attention to how big the pile gets. If a stack gets too bulky, subdivide it. For example, "School Records" can be broken down by each individual child.

## File According to Usage & Alphabet

☞ Seldom-needed files (old tax returns, insurance policies) can go in the back of the drawer. Files you use often (checking account, bills) go toward the front.

☞ To help figure out where to file each piece of paper, consider how you will use it. A Caribbean travel brochure should be filed under "Vacation Ideas," not "Caribbean." (Don't save the brochure at all if you plan on never leaving your hometown.)

☞ Be specific — but not too specific, or you'll end up with a lot of skinny files. Are you saving an article on how to fix a leaky faucet? File it under "Household Repairs," not "Leaky Faucet."

☞ Begin file headings with nouns rather than adjectives: "Job Applications — Current," not "Current Job Applications."

☞ Ask yourself what word would first enter your mind if you were searching for the information. The test of the system is to be able to retrieve something.

☞ Make a file index — an alphabetical list of all your file headings — and update it every few months.

**Problem:** Too much stuff. (Research shows that 80 percent of the material in most files is never used.)
**Solution:** Get a wastebasket. (If you generate a lot of recyclable paper, get two.) This philosophy is also known as "When in doubt, toss it out."

If keeping things for a rainy day is ingrained in your character, ask yourself, "What is the worst thing that could happen if I threw this away?" If the answer is "Nothing much," throw it out. (Note: There are definitely items you need to keep — and we'll give you that list.)

If you're not using something, get rid of it. (Notice the present tense.) Ask yourself, "How long has it been since I've used it?" "Do I need this many?" If you want to save magazines or newspapers, stash only those that fit in a single basket or in a stack on one shelf. Clip and file useful articles, then recycle the rest of the magazine. (Did you know that as of September 1991, there were approximately 3,784 billion copies of *National Geographic* in print, and just about every one of them is still in somebody's basement?)

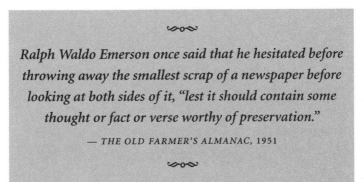

Reduce unwanted mail at the source. If you want to eliminate your name from national advertising lists, send your name, address, and ZIP code to this address:
Mail Preference Service
Direct Marketing Association
11 W. 42nd Street
P.O. Box 3861
New York, NY 10163-3861. (Include commonly used variations in the spelling of your name and the format of your address.)

Don't handle paper over and over again. When you open mail, don't leave it lying on top of the counter. Sort it into four categories: "To Do," "To File," "To Pay," and "Toss." "Toss" goes in the trash — now.

*Ralph Waldo Emerson once said that he hesitated before throwing away the smallest scrap of a newspaper before looking at both sides of it, "lest it should contain some thought or fact or verse worthy of preservation."*

— *THE OLD FARMER'S ALMANAC,* 1951

# WHAT TO SAVE (FOR A WHILE OR FOREVER)

✔ Keep canceled checks that substantiate tax deductions or major purchases. Pull out these checks when you get your bank statement each month. File tax-related checks under "Taxes" (charitable giving, medical expenses); file big-purchase checks with product warranties.

✔ Keep a file with purchase-and-sale documents (including IRS Form 2119) for every home you've owned.

✔ Keep a file of capital home-improvement expenditures. This will *increase* the home's cost for tax purposes, thereby *decreasing* your capital gain later. Routine repairs and maintenance don't count; a new roof, a remodeled kitchen or bath, and landscaping do.)

✔ Keep credit card records for six years.

✔ Keep health records forever.

✔ Keep contracts for seven years past the expiration date.

✔ Keep loan papers for three years after final payment.

✔ Keep records of all contributions to nondeductible IRAs, including Form 8606.

✔ Keep records of investments, with separate files for each mutual fund or brokerage account.

✔ Wills: Don't put your will in a safe-deposit box; many states limit access when the holder dies. Keep a copy at home and leave the original with your attorney. Destroy outdated versions.

✔ Tax returns: At the end of the tax season, save copies of federal and state returns and all supporting documents in a single folder. Store six years' worth. The IRS has three years to examine your return, six if you have substantially underreported your income.

## WHAT YOU CAN SAFELY THROW AWAY*

✔ Expired insurance policies (with no possibility of a claim).

✔ Non-tax-related checks more than three years old.

✔ Records for items you no longer own (cars, boats).

✔ Pay stubs going back more than two years.

(*Note: If you are not sure about whether you should save a particular item, consult your accountant or lawyer first.)

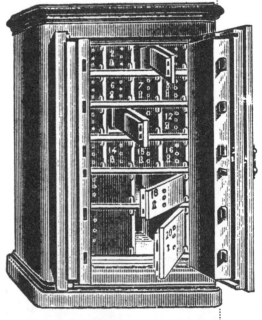

## WHAT TO KEEP IN A SAFE-DEPOSIT BOX

✔ Photocopy valuable, hard-to-replace papers. Place originals in a safe-deposit box and keep photocopies at home with a list of safe-deposit contents.

✔ Deeds and other records of ownership. Include material that documents the condition of your home: written inventory, appraisals, photos, receipts.

✔ Birth and marriage certificates.

✔ Passports.

✔ Stock and bond certificates.

✔ List of all insurance policies and agents (store actual documents at home).

✔ Adoption papers.

✔ Divorce decrees.

✔ Custody agreements.

# What to Do with the Stuff You Usually Throw Away

**Banana skins.** Puree in a food processor and use to polish silver.

**Bones.** Boil to make stock, then use power tools to cut them into buttons and beads.

**Bottle caps.** Nail to a piece of wood, fluted sides up, and use them to scrape scales from fish.

**Sardine can keys.** Attach them to the bottom of toothpaste tubes and roll the tube up from the bottom, thus gaining an extra week's worth of paste.

**Cigarette butts.** Soak leftover tobacco in water overnight, then use the water on your plants to kill mealybugs.

**Coffee grounds.** Dry the grounds in a warm oven, then sprinkle in the litter box or set a canful in the refrigerator to absorb odors.

**Old combs.** Use to hold small nails and avoid smashing your fingers.

**Corncobs.** Dried corncobs make good scrubbers for especially dirty jobs.

**Roll-on deodorant bottles.** Can be refilled with bath oil, liquid starch, suntan lotion, water for moistening stamps and envelopes, or paint for kids.

**Egg cartons.** Make good ice cube trays and starter pots for spring seedlings, or you can nail lots of them to a wall, overlapping the tops and the cups, for insulation.

**Eggshells.** Remove stains from china and glassware by soaking them in a vinegar-and-eggshell bath.

**Hair.** Makes good fertilizer, with 16 times the nitrogen in cow manure.

**Old light bulbs.** Dip in metallic paint, twist a thin piece of wire around the metal grooves, and you have a Christmas tree ornament.

**Styrofoam meat trays.** Draw the outline of your foot on one, cut it out with a razor blade, and slip it into winter boots for insulation.

**Plastic milk jugs.** Cut out the bottom and use the jugs as heat-retaining caps for garden plants in spring and fall.

**Used motor oil.** Soak the ends of fence posts or tomato stakes in the oil for 24 hours to make them waterproof.

**Old records.** Heat in a 350° F oven or plunge into very hot water to mold into snack bowls or bookends.

**Worn-out gloves.** Cut off the fingertips, make a pair of slits for a belt, and you have a holder for screwdrivers.

# Dry & Cool, or How to Keep Things Fresh

*BY CYNTHIA VAN HAZINGA*

There's a good reason the Dead Sea Scrolls survived in an underground cave. Dry and cool is the basic rule for storing most things. These are the conditions that postpone the deterioration of tissue by infection from foreign microbes such as bacteria or molds (their spores are everywhere!) or by self-destruction from its own metabolic processes. Deterioration is inevitable, but it can be delayed and minimized. In arranging safe storage for the necessities of life, man — and woman — has shown great imagination.

A few basic guidelines: Find a place for everything — and keep everything in its place. One rotten apple *does* spoil the barrel; control the mold population by tossing out any moldy fruits or vegetables and clean storage containers thoroughly from time to time.

Cool temperatures slow the biochemical activity of cells without killing them. Refrigerators are cool, but they're not dry (and not wet enough, either, for some storage); cupboards are dry, but they may not be cool. There's a lot to be said for the old-fashioned root cellar — the dug-out, underground variety common before refrigerators, where country folk kept potatoes and other root crops. In northern states, the winter temperature in a root cellar can be kept just above 32° F, which is best for storing most vegetables, and the humidity can be controlled by letting in fresh air. Keep your bountiful harvest well into the winter by using dark, unheated places in your house. Utilize the space along the basement stairs, under the bulkhead, in the attic, or even under beds or in closets of an unheated spare room. Or partition one corner of an unheated basement, insulate it, and install a door and a thermometer.

Apples   To store a harvest of apples or other fall fruits and vegetables, you may want to improvise a root cellar, perhaps in an unheated space protected from freezing or by insulating the bulkhead doors over cellar stairs. Remember that fruits and vegetables need an occasional change of air — after all, they're still alive and breathing. You give them oxygen when you open the bulkhead or the cellar door from the outside, and in cold weather you may let in a bit of heat from the cellar side. Apples keep well for about six months at temperatures between 32° and 45° F. Even a simple Styrofoam chest or a double cardboard box can approximate root cellar conditions.

Batteries,   Store these in a cool, dry place, out of reach of rodents and
Candles,   children. Professional photographers often keep their film in
Film &   the refrigerator, but only when it's tightly sealed in a mois-
Soap   ture-proof wrap.

Berries   Never rinse berries before storage; doing so washes off the thin, protective epidermal layer. Store them in a cool, dry place; refrigeration favors the growth of mold as a result of condensation on the surface. (This is why most small fruits keep only a day or two in the refrigerator.)

**Bread**

Put bread in a breadbox. Staling is a temperature-dependent process that proceeds most rapidly at temperatures just above freezing and very slowly below freezing. What's going on is retrogradation of the starch molecules — molecular reordering that makes the starch and protein phases more dense and more segregated from water; not simple drying out, but a change in the location and distribution of water molecules. Frozen bread keeps well as a result of the leveling off of the decline in its water-holding capacity. In one experiment, bread stored at 46° F (a typical refrigerator temperature) staled as much in one day as bread kept at 86° F did in six. So if you're going to freeze bread, freeze it fast; otherwise, store it wrapped at room temperature.

**Cut Flowers**

Keep them in a cool spot in water conditioned with a packaged floral preservative or one home-brewed with sugar (to replace the glucose the flowers are losing), citric acid such as lemon juice (to lower the pH), and carbonation or a bit of household bleach (to slow the growth of bacteria). Cut flowers last longer if their stems are cut with a sharp blade, either underwater or seconds before being plunged into water. The water should be warmish, never cold.

**Drugs &
Remedies**
Ironically, the worst place to keep medicines may be in the over-the-sink bathroom medicine cabinet. Drugs and remedies should be kept cool and dry; bathrooms are often warm and steamy. Store medicines and cosmetics in a dry spot, perhaps a bedroom cabinet.

**Fine China**
Display irreplaceable items in a glass-front cabinet or hard-to-reach shelf, preferably one with a lip to prevent china from "walking" off the edge. Stack same-size plates with a piece of felt between them in piles of about four or six. Don't stack cups or bowls that can crack under the weight. Consider using cup hooks.

**Fish &
Shellfish**
Store fish on ice, briefly. Store shellfish such as clams, mussels, and oysters in cool, well-ventilated boxes, not in airtight plastic bags or containers.

**Fresh
Herbs**
Most fresh herbs (and greens) will keep best when refrigerated unwashed in tightly sealed plastic bags with enough moisture available to prevent wilting. Dill and parsley should be stored with stems immersed in a glass of water tented with a plastic bag. Instead of getting slimy, they will keep for about two weeks. Extended storage of any living tissue in a plastic bag is not advisable; denying the plant cells oxygen makes them switch to anaerobic respiration, build up alcohol, and turn brown. Moisture- and gas-permeable paper and cellophane are better for the long run.

**Grains &
Flours**
Keep "dry" ingredients dry and cool in an airtight, moisture-tight container. Beans, pasta, rice, and other grains store well in tin or plastic, but beans do stale and toughen. Use them up! Prevent vermin or insects from hatching in flour or grains by freezing for a few hours before storage.

**Hockey Pucks & Other Sports Stuff**

We are told that avid Canadian hockey players deep-freeze their pucks so that they move faster when they hit the ice. A tennis player we know admits that he keeps his tennis balls in the refrigerator for the same reason. The size of your freezer may be a consideration. Our freezer is full of coffee beans, cranberries, nuts, vegetable stock, and ice cream, but keep your hockey pucks there if your children are cutting seconds off their scores.

**Mushrooms**

Remove any market wrap and keep them in the refrigerator in a paper bag. The bag will absorb some of the moisture and keep the mushrooms from spoiling.

**Onions**

Mature, dry-skinned onions like it cool and dry. French-braided onions are handy and free to get some ventilation as well.

**Potatoes, Beets, Carrots & Other Root Crops**

See "Apples" or store in a dark, cool place. Unlike berries, these sturdy vegetables should be brushed clean; the soil that clings to them harbors microbes. Never keep potatoes in the refrigerator; at temperatures lower than 40° F, their starch will turn to sugar, making them taste strangely sweet. Don't store apples and potatoes together; the apples give off ethylene gas, which will spoil the potatoes.

Keep other root crops at around 35° to 40° F with high humidity. Set out pans of water to increase moisture. Clipping the tops off parsnips, carrots, beets, and turnips will nip their tendency to use moisture in leafy growth. Store carrots, turnips, or parsnips in boxes of sand. To keep carrots in the refrigerator, wash them right after harvest, remove the tops, and seal in plastic bags.

**Pumpkins & Winter Squash**

Squash don't like to be quite as cool as root crops do. They prefer a temperature of about 50° to 65° F. If you have a coolish bedroom, stashing them under the bed works well.

**Sugar**

Granulated sugar must be kept dry and cool, or it will harden. Brown sugar contains moisture and hardens when exposed to air. Store brown sugar in an airtight container or freezer for extended storage. If it does solidify, it can be softened by exposing it to moisture. Try baking it, covered, at 200° F next to (but not with) a cup of water for about 20 minutes. Or store it with a slice of apple or a citrus rind, tightly enclosed, until it's soft again.

**Tomatoes & Other Tropicals**

Never, ever refrigerate fresh tomatoes. Doing so will ruin their flavor and texture at once. Don't keep them on a sunny windowsill either. A cool room temperature is best.

Ripe tomatoes, which are basically tropical fruits, and other fruits native to warm climates do not keep well in the cold. Bananas turn black, avocados stop softening, and citrus fruits get spotty. Think of the country of origin and store these fruits, as well as pineapples, melons, eggplant, cucumbers, peppers, and beans, at about 50° F if possible.

**Your Wedding Dress**

Any important textile calls for acid-free paper and boxes (available from dry cleaners). Wood pulp disintegrates and takes the fabric with it.

# IN PRAISE OF THE PANTRY

The kitchen of the old New England farmhouse was always the hub of the home, and traditionally it had seven doors. One of those doors led to a pantry large enough to store all the groceries and food in everyday use (except for milk, butter, and cheese, which were usually stored separately). As settlement moved west, the custom of the pantry, or larder, moved with it. Often the pantry and kitchen were located in a wing or ell off the main building — a design seen in farmhouse after farmhouse across the Midwest.

Whenever possible, the pantry was located on the north side of the house, with a north-facing window and a door to close it off from the warm kitchen. In an age without easy refrigeration, that north-facing window could be adjusted to provide just the right amount of ventilation to keep food cool but not frozen from October to April. Grains, sugar, spices, herbs, salt, knives, candles, matches, and jars and crocks of preserves all had the same need for cool, dry storage conditions.

The pantry is still as functional as ever, a place to store provisions, the family silver, a large bag of dog food, the holiday punch bowl and platters, those jars of strawberry jam you canned on a warm day last June, and the oil lamps you use when the power goes out in a snowstorm. And if the pantry has a north-facing window, all the better.

∽o∾

*The true economy of housekeeping is simply the art of
gathering up all the fragments, so that nothing be lost. I
mean fragments of time, as well as materials. Nothing
should be thrown away as long as it is possible to make any
use of it, however trifling that use may be.*

— LYDIA MARIA CHILD (1802–1880)

∽o∾

## HINTS & SUGGESTIONS

### Tidying Up

☞ Put old bookcases in closets for organized storage. This works great in children's rooms.

☞ Use shoe boxes inside dresser drawers as dividers for underwear, stockings, and other small items.

☞ Make a small lost-and-found box to keep in a convenient place in your house for all the little things you find in odd places.

☞ Wait one year before throwing out a piece of clothing. If you haven't worn it in a year, you'll never miss it.

☞ Keep a few extra folders at the back of your file cabinet so that it will be easy to start a new file when you need to.

☞ Use different-colored plastic baskets with handles to store frozen foods in a chest-type freezer. Keep all "like" items together in one basket — for example, vegetables in one, beef in another. Then make a list of colors and categories and keep it near the freezer. This saves having to dig into the freezer to find what you want.

# Chapter 2

# The Handy Homeowner,

## or Knowing When It's Time to Call the Professionals

*A tool knows exactly how it is meant to be handled, while the user of the tool can only have an approximate idea.*

— *MILAN KUNDERA (b. 1929)*

THERE'S NO GETTING AROUND IT: IF YOU OWN A HOME, you need an assortment of simple tools, the skills to go with them, and a willingness to haul them out from time to time and do whatever it is that needs doing. Some homeowners actually enjoy taking on an occasional repair or construction project. Even if you're not one of them — and the following pretty much assumes that you're not — you really have very little choice. A great many jobs simply won't be done unless you do them yourself.

Imagine, for example, that you want to attach a wooden spice shelf to your kitchen wall within easy reach of the stove but don't feel capable of doing the job yourself. Can't you just call Zeke, the kindly, efficient handyman who used do odd jobs for Dick and Jane's family?

Well, you could, but you don't know his last name, and he's probably retired by now anyway. You could try calling XYZ Construction and asking them to send a carpenter over to your house, but you might as well try getting a hand surgeon to drop over to trim your cuticles.

Realistically, you have three options. The first is to abandon the spice shelf idea altogether, rationalizing the decision on the grounds that cooking experts recommend against storing spices too near the stove, where they tend to dry out and lose their flavor.

The second option is to come up with a more substantial project — something along the lines of a four-room addition off the south side of the house, including a sunspace, hot-tub room, and sculpture studio — that the good folks at XYZ Construction will find profitable enough to bother with. Then, when it's almost done and the builders are packing up to leave, you can assume an offhand "oh, by the way" manner and bring out the spice shelf.

But that's an expensive and roundabout solution at best. And at worst, it won't work. Professional builders hate those kinds of small,

fussy jobs, even when they're already in the house working on something else. They'll probably tell you they don't have the right kind of screws, pile into the company truck to go get some, and never come back.

That, of course, leaves the third option — to screw up your courage and tackle the job on your own. If you're new at this sort of thing, you'll soon encounter an odd paradox: it's much harder to obtain information about small, simple projects than it is to learn about large, complex ones. That's because the large, complex tasks — things like building a grandfather clock, pouring a concrete foundation, laying a hardwood floor, or reshingling a roof — have been thoroughly described and analyzed in countless books and magazines. Anyone who can read and follow directions can have a crack at these projects, given the ability to drive nails, saw a board to a penciled line, and perform a few other basic tasks.

The skills you need to perform those tasks are harder to pin down. Although they're easily passed from one person to another, they're nearly impossible to reduce to writing. A really complete treatise on screwdriver use, for example, would have to begin with a working definition of the difference between clockwise and counterclockwise — a job for a metaphysician, not a how-to writer. Even the most exhaustive how-to text must assume that the reader knows something. If you lack that assumed knowledge, you're out of luck as far as the written word goes. You'll just have to get someone to show you.

But that's not so hard — is it? Actually, yes, it's very hard for some of us. By the time we've traveled far enough through life to own a home, we tend to think of ourselves as mature, serious adults who know our way around. We're worldly, knowledgeable people, and we'd much rather think about the impressive variety of things we do know than about those few things we don't know.

And we certainly don't want to admit that among those few things are one or two trifling skills — the ability to drive a few wood screws through a spice shelf and into a wall stud, say — that many people learned in childhood. Anyway, we just don't have time for such things these days. Why, we're going to have to work evenings and weekends as it is to pay XYZ Construction for that four-room addition.

Of course, you probably don't have that problem yourself. But it's a safe bet that you know someone — or several someones — who do. It's so common, in fact, that it sustains a small but significant sector of our national economy, as you can see for yourself by cruising the aisles of any large building-supply store.

Mixed in with the ordinary, workaday building materials made to be used by those who know what they're doing — things like dimension lumber, nails, paint, copper piping, and so on — you'll find an assortment of products designed specifically for those who can't or won't learn anything new but want to put their personal stamp on their home. These products include things such as fake press-on brick, embossed plastic floor tiles, and wood-grain paneling that can be tacked up with a stapler. Their implicit promise is that skill just doesn't matter — and in one sense, at least, it's a promise that rarely goes unfulfilled. Even when the installation of such products is badly bungled, the results aren't much worse than if it had been done properly.

> *The contents of any package that prominently features the word* handyman *should be considered highly suspect.*

Fortunately, such products are easy to identify and avoid. The contents of any package that prominently features the word *handyman* should be considered highly suspect. Other warning signs include promiscuous use of the word *beautify* or an overemphasis on ease of installation, especially if the project is said to be "a breeze," "a snap," or "a cinch." Finally, it pays to be skeptical of anything advertised as "perfect for home or office" — a phrase that strongly suggests that the manufacturer just couldn't think of anything substantial to say about it.

It would be easy to condemn the people who make such things as unprincipled rascals. But while commerce has always been good at pandering to our worst instincts, it doesn't create them out of thin air. As much as we'd all like to get something for nothing, we have only ourselves to blame if we let that desire lead us into making foolish choices. If you want good work, you have to expect to pay for it.

That's not to say that quality work necessarily costs more money. Even in the short run, the nice wooden spice shelf will probably cost less than the cheapjack wood-grain version with the self-adhesive back, suitable for home or office. You'll pay for its higher quality indirectly — by spending some time learning to do the job right, and a bit more time actually doing it.

Ultimately, most worthwhile home improvements also demand something in the way of self-improvement. This takes time and commitment, and it may not always go as smoothly as you might wish.

Don't expect to do your best work the first time. Professional builders have the luxury of refining their skills on other people's houses while getting paid for it. You have only your own house to practice on. In many cases, you'll just be getting good at a given task as you finish it — allowing you to contemplate the evidence of your early lack of skill forever after. And no matter how good you get, that will help keep you humble.

# When to Call In the Pros

**Do-It-Yourself Jobs**

☞ Jobs with inexpensive tools and materials, such as indoor painting.

☞ "Grunt" work, which involves more sweat than materials, such as removing paint, wallpaper, or tiles.

☞ Jobs that require few skills, such as patching holes in walls, caulking windows, and yard work.

**Jobs to Hire Out**

☞ Electrical, plumbing, and foundation work that must pass building codes. A licensed professional will know local requirements.

☞ Projects with expensive building materials, such as hand-painted tile or high-end carpeting.

☞ Dangerous jobs, such as installing a new roof.

*I have measured my life with coffee spoons.*
— *THOMAS STEARNS ELIOT (1888–1965)*

# How Long Is a Furrow?  *BY WINIFRED H. SCHEIB*

How long is a furrow? Ask this question of an experienced Yankee farmer, and he'll probably drawl, "Well, that depends." Yet in the English system of measurement, which we Americans inherited, the length of a furrow was established at 220 yards by decree of the Tudor kings, and a furrow-long became a furlong, or one-eighth of a mile.

Today we accept many common units of measurement without realizing that they exist because some early ruler pronounced that they would be so. Take the foot, for example; this basic measurement is based on the length of the human foot. There are a lot of corns and bunions around as testimony to the fact that human feet vary considerably in size, so it was usually the chieftain's foot that determined the standard. Thus it was also with the inch, originally a thumb's breadth, depending on who was under who's thumb.

"Make yourself an ark," God instructed Noah, "three hundred cubits long, fifty cubits wide, and thirty cubits high."

Noah, as we are all aware, was quite willing to get busy on an ark, but how long was a cubit? It turned out to be the distance from the elbow to the tip of the middle finger, and as long as Noah was boss of the construction project, he undoubtedly used his own body measurements, the result being that a cubit came to be about 18 inches.

Measurements went along in this haphazard fashion for centuries, and many tribal wars possibly were caused because one leader's foot was longer than that of some equally powerful rival's. The Romans, however, were great organizers, and they needed some standardized system to keep the empire in line. They insisted that the mile be defined as 1,000 paces, a pace being 5 Roman feet, an easy double step for a lusty Roman legionary.

As conquerors do, the Romans introduced this 5,000-foot mile into Britain. That probably would be the distance of our mile today if it had not been for Queen Elizabeth I. In her reign, it was decided that this Roman mile was most inconvenient in England, as it failed to accommodate our old friend the furlong. By statute of the queen, the mile was increased to 5,280 feet so that 8 furlongs would fit neatly into it.

English royalty was a domineering lot when it came to measurements. Tradition says that it was Henry I who decreed that the yard should be the distance from the tip of his nose to the end of his thumb, a measurement still beloved by Yankee housewives at yardage counters. The Saxon kings had previously been content to consider a yard as being the length of the girdle around the waist. Perhaps Henry I was slimmer through the middle than his predecessors and used his prerogative to change the yard for some kingly gain.

At any rate, this was the case with Charles I of England, when he decided to increase his revenues with a tax on milk, honey, and wine as measured by the "jack" or "jackpot." Not only did he impose the tax, but he also reduced the size of the jack, which was half a gill of four fluid ounces. The old nursery rhyme about Jack and Jill is believed to be a 17th-century protest song against this royal skullduggery, for if the jack fell in value, would not the gill come tumbling after?

In matters involving taxation, this flexibility of measurement almost always worked out to the ruler's advantage. The acre, for example, was, in British tradition, the amount of land a man could plow in a day with a team of oxen. Obviously, much maneuvering was possible here, as an acre would vary according to the type of terrain as well as the ambition of the farmer and his animals. With such imprecise standards, it's no wonder the poor farmer found it hard to buy shoes for his children.

When it came to shoes, the nobility naturally had the best chance of being well shod, yet it may have been a farmer who decided that footwear should be measured by the length of a barleycorn. If you wore a size 12, your shoes were 12 barleycorns long, and each full size was one barleycorn longer than the preceding one. Though much barleycorn has long since been diverted to the manufacture of whiskey and malt liquors, we are still measuring shoes by barleycorns. If you don't believe this, ask your shoe man if your size 12 isn't one-third inch longer than a size 11. That's a barleycorn, John.

The measurement whims of English royalty were transplanted to New England with the British colonists. Today most American units roughly parallel the British ones. That is, they did. In recent years, Britain elected to join most of the rest of the world in using metric measurements, and, as the other Commonwealth countries follow suit, the United States will be alone in conforming to a system largely evolved by the dictates of long-dead royalty.

If most of our early colonists had been French instead of English, our own schoolchildren would not be droning through arbitrary tables about how many inches go into a yard, how many ounces into a gallon, or how many pounds into a ton. The practical French adopted the metric system back in 1791, thereby guaranteeing their offspring freedom from all but decimal fractions thenceforth. The logical terminology of the metric system applies whether the units are of length, weight, volume, or electrical output; a "kilo" always means a thousand, whether it is meters, grams, liters, or watts.

Many people are now wondering whether measurements that were good enough for the "in-group" in ancient times are not archaic in the era of computers, space exploration, and international trade. Conversion to the metric system would be expensive for American manufacturers and require a drastic change of habit by all of us Yankees.

If you could ask the opinion of one of the Tudor kings, he might reply, "In these times, our English measures can't survive fur long."

# ORIGINS OF OLD-TIME (PREMETRIC) MEASURING UNITS

**Foot.** The length of Charlemagne's foot, modified in 1305 to be 36 barleycorns laid end to end.

**Inch.** The width across the knuckle on King Edgar's thumb, or, obviously, 3 barleycorns.

**Yard.** The reach from King Henry I's nose to his royal fingertips, a distance also twice as long as a cubit.

**Cubit.** The length of the arm from elbow to fingertip.

**Mile.** One thousand double steps of a Roman legionary. Later, Queen Bess added more feet so that the mile would equal 8 furlongs.

**Furlong.** The length of a furrow a team of oxen could plow before resting.

**Acre.** The amount of land a yoke of oxen would plow in one day.

**Fathom.** The span of a seaman's outstretched arms; 880 fathoms make a mile.

The metric system uses the meter, defined precisely as 1,650,763.73 wavelengths of orange-red light emitted by the krypton-86 atom, or originally one-ten-millionth the length of the longitude from the North Pole to the equator. The meter is exactly 39.37 inches — or some 118 barleycorns.

## MAKESHIFT MEASURERS

When you don't have a measuring stick or tape, use what is at hand. To this list, add any other items that you always (or nearly always) have handy.

|                                | IN INCHES |
| ------------------------------ | --------- |
| Credit card                    | $3\frac{3}{8} \times 2\frac{1}{8}$ |
| Business card (standard)       | $3\frac{1}{2} \times 2$ |
| Dollar bill                    | $6\frac{1}{8} \times 2\frac{5}{8}$ |
| Quarter (diameter)             | 1 |
| Penny (diameter)               | $\frac{3}{4}$ |
| Ballpoint pen                  | $5\frac{1}{2}$ |
| Videotape cassette             | $7\frac{3}{4} \times 4$ |
| *The Old Farmer's Almanac*     | $5\frac{1}{4} \times 8$ |

CUSTOM MEASUREMENTS

| | |
| --- | --- |
| Your foot/shoe | _____ |
| Your outstretched arms (fingertip to fingertip) | _____ |
| Your hand (palm width) | _____ |
| Your hand (base of palm to tip of middle finger) | _____ |
| Your outstretched hand (thumb tip to pinkie tip) | _____ |

# METRIC CONVERSION

| CONVENTIONAL TO METRIC, MULTIPLY BY | | METRIC TO CONVENTIONAL, MULTIPLY BY | |
|---|---|---|---|
| inch | 2.54 | centimeter | 0.39 | inch |
| foot | 30.48 | centimeter | 0.033 | foot |
| yard | 0.91 | meter | 1.09 | yard |
| mile | 1.61 | kilometer | 0.62 | mile |
| square inch | 6.45 | square centimeter | 0.15 | square inch |
| square foot | 0.09 | square meter | 10.76 | square foot |
| square yard | 0.8 | square meter | 1.2 | square yard |
| square mile | 0.84 | square kilometer | 0.39 | square mile |
| acre | 0.4 | hectare | 2.47 | acre |
| ounce | 28.0 | gram | 0.035 | ounce |
| pound | 0.45 | kilogram | 2.2 | pound |
| short ton (2,000 pounds) | 0.91 | metric ton | 1.10 | short ton |
| ounce | 30.0 | milliliter | 0.034 | ounce |
| pint | 0.47 | liter | 2.1 | pint |
| quart | 0.95 | liter | 1.06 | quart |
| gallon | 3.8 | liter | 0.26 | gallon |

If you know the conventional measurement and want to convert it to metric, multiply it by the number in the first column (example: 1 inch equals 2.54 centimeters). If you know the metric measurement, multiply it by the number in the second column (example: 2 meters equals 2.18 yards).

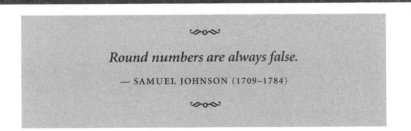

*Round numbers are always false.*

— SAMUEL JOHNSON (1709–1784)

*Man is a tool-using animal....*
*Without tools he is nothing, with tools he is all.*
— THOMAS CARLYLE (1795–1881)

# HOMEOWNER'S TOOL KIT

**The Essentials**
- ✔ Butt chisel
- ✔ Putty knife
- ✔ Adjustable wrench
- ✔ Slip-joint pliers
- ✔ Needle-nose pliers
- ✔ Block plane
- ✔ Four-in-one rasp
- ✔ Hacksaw
- ✔ Crosscut saw
- ✔ Retractable steel ruler
- ✔ Drain auger
- ✔ C-clamp
- ✔ Nail set
- ✔ Curved-claw hammer
- ✔ Push drill and drill point
- ✔ 3 standard screwdrivers (3 sizes)
- ✔ 2 Phillips screwdrivers (2 sizes)
- ✔ Combination square
- ✔ Level
- ✔ Utility knife
- ✔ Toilet plunger
- ✔ Screws and nails

**Other Supplies**
- ✔ Machine oil
- ✔ Penetrating lubricant
- ✔ Pencils
- ✔ Bolts and nuts, hollow-wall fasteners, etc.
- ✔ Adhesives
- ✔ Sandpaper and steel wool
- ✔ Sharpening stone
- ✔ Wire brush
- ✔ Paintbrushes
- ✔ Dustpan and brush
- ✔ Lint-free rags or cheesecloth
- ✔ Clip-on light
- ✔ Grounded extension cord
- ✔ Single-edge razor blades with holder
- ✔ Scissors
- ✔ Toolbox
- ✔ Stepladder

# Up Against the Wallpaper

*BY KENNETH M. SHELDON*

The first step in wallpapering is to determine how much paper you need. There's a simple formula for figuring this out that anyone with a degree in calculus can explain to you. Or you can ask a salesperson in a home-decorating store for help.

He or she will ask you for the dimensions of the room and how many windows and doors it has. (Having this figure in hand will really impress the clerk.) The salesperson will scribble some figures on a piece of paper, mumble a few magic words, and say, "Eight double rolls."

If you ask for an explanation of the calculations, the salesperson will look annoyed, cover the paper with something like a cross between Einstein's theory of relativity and Knute Rockne's Statue of Liberty play, and come up with a different figure. When it comes to rigorous application of scientific principles, this is right up there with dowsing for water and the flat-earth theory.

At any rate, you should always buy more wallpaper than you think you will need, for several reasons:

**1.** You'll be wrong.

**2.** You can always use what's left over as industrial-strength wrapping paper.

**3.** It's insurance. You should always keep the leftover wallpaper on hand to repair later rips and tears. Not that you'll ever need the leftover paper. In fact, when you move, you will probably have 112 partial rolls of old wallpaper in the attic, none of them touched since the day you put up the paper. But if you throw the extra paper away, I guarantee you will need

---

∞o∞

*I live in my house as I live inside my skin: I know more beautiful, more ample, more sturdy and more picturesque skins; but it would seem to me unnatural to exchange them for mine.*

— PRIMO LEVI (1919–1987)

∞o∞

it the next week. This is the Universal Rule of Throwing Things Out.

## Off with the Old...

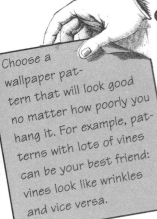

Choose a wallpaper pattern that will look good no matter how poorly you hang it. For example, patterns with lots of vines can be your best friend: vines look like wrinkles and vice versa.

You can remove old wallpaper in a number of ways. These methods involve applying liberal doses of steam, chemicals, or curses, all of which are about equally ineffective. In the end, you will probably have to scrape the old paper off with a putty knife. If your putty knife, like mine, is not likely to be found by anyone in this or the next several generations, you'll have to buy a new one. Buy a cheap one, because it is probably going to join the other one, wherever it is that old putty knives go to die.

### Purchasing Supplies

At one time, you could go to the hardware store, ask for a bucket, a brush, and some wallpaper paste, and you were ready to wallpaper. Today there are about 50 different kinds of wallpaper paste for regular paper or vinyl paper, cellulose paste, wheat paste, premixed paste, organic paste, and paste with genuine NutraSweet.

Then there's sizing, which is something you put on the walls to make the paper stick better. You may have thought that that was the purpose of the paste. This is a common mistake. Just don't exhibit your ignorance about these matters to the salespeople — they already figure that you don't know what you're doing. Instead, march up to the display of wallpaper supplies, grab a package of paste (any paste), a package of sizing, a pasting brush, and one of those long, flat brushes for smoothing out lumps.

The salesclerk may try to sell you a lot of other equipment, such as a seam roller, a cutting edge, mixing buckets, and so on. While not absolutely necessary, these can be helpful, and you'll have plenty of time to look them over depending on where your spouse has wandered off to.

### Hanging the Wallpaper

Before you begin wallpapering, take everything out of the room except your supplies. Otherwise, by the time you get done, everything will be covered with dried paste and bits of wallpaper, which are very hard to remove from furniture, pets, and small children. You might want to spread plastic over your rug (although wallpaper bits might add an interesting effect to an Oriental).

The first step in applying the paper is cutting it to the right length. You need to leave a little extra paper at the top and bottom of each piece so that you can move it up or down to make the pattern match the preceding piece. But you can't waste too much paper, or you might run out.

You'll need a large, flat surface on which to lay the paper while spreading paste on it. Or you can use prepasted paper, which has little globules of dried paste that come alive when you dunk it in water. Usually, this is just enough paste to make the paper stick to itself, to you, and to anything else it touches — except the wall. If you really want that paper to stay put, slap on some regular paste. Otherwise, the first time you walk into the room after the traumatic wallpapering experience, the paper may be so glad to see you that it falls into your arms.

For prepasted paper, you'll also need one of those long plastic trays to soak it in. After about the third piece of wallpaper, these trays invariably develop a crack in one of the corners and dribble water all over your floor. Stick a piece of bubble gum over the crack and keep going.

The first piece of wallpaper that you put up should be plumb (that is, straight up and down), or all the other pieces will be cockeyed, too. Fruit patterns may look all right this way, but birds will look as if they're kamikazes attacking one corner of the room.

Speaking of corners, never start wallpapering near one. If the part of the wallpaper that will come after the corner is wider than the part that comes before it, cut a narrow strip that barely goes around the corner and then start with a new strip. Put a floor-to-ceiling cupboard in that corner. Tear down the wall and move it back. Do anything, but don't try to paper the wall as it is. Whatever you do, don't try to wallpaper around a corner with your spouse. Divorce statistics are high enough as it is.

By the way, the ability to wallpaper together is a good test of whether a couple

Once you've got the paper on the wall, you may notice little bubbles of air that you'll have to smooth out. Here's a trick I learned: stick a pin in the bubbles and squeeze out the excess air. Or just wait. Like pimples, the bubbles sometimes disappear with maturity as the paste dries and the paper shrinks. Until then, work on developing your room's personality.

belong together. Any couple considering marriage should be locked in a room with a selection of wallpaper and the necessary equipment. If, when you open the door, both people are still alive — regardless of how the room looks — they can get married.

After the piece of wallpaper is where you want it, you'll need to trim off the excess at the top and bottom. You can trim the paper while it is still wet — which is like slicing a wet lasagna noodle with a screwdriver held at arm's length — or you can trim the paper after it dries, thereby pulling the paint off the ceiling and the mopboard where the paper has stuck to them. Either way, trimming will be easier if you use a sharp, new razor blade, not the one you've had for years and used to scrape paint from the windows, open UPS packages, and adjust the tiny screws in your glasses.

## Finishing Up

The rest is easy. Proceed around the room, use lots of paste, clean up, and then hang loud pictures over anything that looks really bad. If the room seems a lot darker than it was before you began, you may have papered over the windows.

*Home's not merely four square walls,*
*Though with pictures hung and gilded;*
*Home is where Affection calls, —*
*filled with shrines the heart hath builded.*

— CHARLES SWAIN (1803–1874)

# Painting Pointers

BY JOHN CROSBY FREEMAN

## 1. Technique: It's All in the Wrist

Resist the old habit of wiping the back of the loaded brush on the rim of the can. All this does is reduce your paint load by 50 percent. Carefully dip the brush no more than half the length of the bristles. Gently tap the front and back of the loaded brush on the wall of the paint can to allow excess paint to drain. Don't start your next loaded brush stroke where you ended the previous one. Begin ahead of it and work back to it. Today's top-quality acrylic latex paints don't require the fussy brushing of old-fashioned oil-based paints. They are chemically engineered to level out with very little help from you. "Flow and go" should be your motto. The more you agitate your acrylic latex paint with excessive brushing, the more likely it is that it will show brush marks.

## 2. Skip the Disposable Brushes

For a serious paint project, the best thing to do with a throwaway brush is to throw it away before you use it. No matter what quality paint you apply, it feels better and looks better with a top-quality brush. It holds a larger load of paint, which translates into fewer visits to the paint pail. It releases paint throughout every stroke. Bargain brushes dump the paint load upon contact with the surface and then smear it. Quality brushes feature longer bristles and more of them. Split ends are bad for your hair, but quality paintbrushes have plenty of them to spread and smooth the paint with a minimum of effort. The best brushes have a heft and balance that make them a pleasure to use. They are "keepers" and will provide you with years of reliable use.

An old trick of the trade is to moisten the brush prior to painting, using water for latex paints and mineral spirits for oil-based paints. Shake out the excess liquid before painting. The paint will release more smoothly throughout the job, and the brush will clean up more easily.

## 3. Painting Vinyl Siding

Top-quality acrylic latex paints stick to vinyl siding like glue. But it's dangerous to paint white siding because any color you apply will be darker and stress the vinyl with solar heat gain. The darker the color, the more likely it

## Working with the Weather

*Exterior Painting* Before you start, read the instructions on the paint can; paints differ in their temperature tolerance. As a general rule, choose weather above 40° F for the best paint flow. Heavy winds can bring dust and debris, as well as make it more difficult to work on a ladder. For your own safety, avoid very hot days unless the house is well shaded.

The weather on the day before you paint is just as important as on the day you paint. It should be above freezing and dry, preferably with a breeze or wind, so that the surface you are painting is completely dry. Never paint after a long wet spell when the wood may be holding moisture that will prevent the paint from adhering properly.

*Interior Painting* Don't repaint windowsills and frames on a cold, windy day or a humid summer day. A dry day in the fifties or low sixties with a light breeze is perfect. While wind will help the paint dry faster, it carries dust, pollen, insects, and whatever other debris lives in the air each season, all of which will stick to the drying paint and mar its surface. The weather should be warm enough to leave the windows open, both for convenience in painting and to keep air circulating so that fumes will dispel and paint will dry.

The same advice holds for painting other interior surfaces. Paint dries too quickly (flowing unevenly) in the dry atmosphere of a winter-heated home, and fumes will pervade a closed house.        — *Barbara Radcliffe Rogers*

is that the vinyl will warp and sag from the heat generated by the color. (Steel or aluminum siding can be painted with acrylic latex in any color without fear of warping.) A gentle and traditional approach to trim and accent colors for a white house is to paint your favorite stone gray on the trim of the roofline, window casings, foundation boards, and porch floors. Then select your favorite deep, dark, delicious accent color for the shutters and doors, perhaps midnight bluegrass (a color I invented), old burgundy, or dark delft blue.

Are you painting your house before selling it? Think seriously about yellow. Real estate professionals from coast to coast report that yellow houses outsell any other color — and seem to move more quickly, too.

## 4. Latex versus Oil

Latex paints have come a long way in the past five to ten years. Top-quality acrylic latex house paints equal the adhesion and durability of ordinary oil-based paints. They are superior in their long-term flexibility, resistance to fading, retention of gloss, and hostility to mildew. They also feature low odor, soap-and-water cleanup, and rapid drying. Acrylic latex paint on walls will resist peeling caused by trapped moisture better than oil-based paint because it is a more permeable coating.

Oil-based paint's resistance to moisture intrusion makes it superior for surfaces subjected to standing water, such as porch floors. And oil-based primer is still the best all-purpose primer for new and old wood. It's also recommended for its ability to bond old paint surfaces that are severely chalking. Two coats of top-quality acrylic latex paint over an oil-based primer is today's best paint system. Incidentally, factory-primed wood doors, windows, and trim should be primed again with an oil-based product to guarantee a superior finish.

## 5. White May Not Be Right

White paint has its use on pristine neoclassical homes in the Georgian, Federal, or general colonial styles. But it's not a cure-all for those who can't decide on anything else. If you have a house with attractive details, it's a tragedy to paint it all white. White is a scissors color because it cuts up walls and detaches the foundation and roof from the walls they support or cap. White also makes any positive color that appears next to it more intense than it really is. As a practical matter, white shows dirt immediately. Visually, it makes your home easy to overlook.

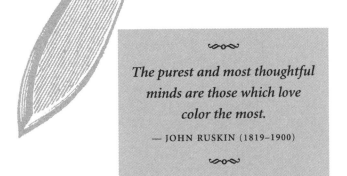

༄

*The purest and most thoughtful
minds are those which love
color the most.*

— JOHN RUSKIN (1819–1900)

༄

# Tricks for Painters

- Before you start painting, rub petroleum jelly or rich hand lotion into all exposed skin for protection and easier cleanup.

- To protect windowpanes, doorknobs, hardware, glass doors, and switch plates, rub them with soap. Paint spatters will settle on the soap and can be washed away when the job is finished.

- Scrunch aluminum foil around door-knobs, thermostats, faucets, and other protrusions before you paint around them. It covers them and stays in place. (Save that crunched aluminum foil for cleaning chrome; just moisten it and rub.)

- To reduce fumes from a new paint job, put a large onion, chopped, in a pail of water in the middle of the room for several hours.

## HINTS & SUGGESTIONS

### Interior Decorating

- Sometimes hardened paintbrushes can be renewed by dipping them in boiling lemon juice. Remove from the heat and let the brush soak for 15 minutes, then wash in soapy water.

- When stenciling, always brush from the outside into the middle. Use less paint rather than more.

- Cut two of the same stencil and use each with a different color.

- You can paint or varnish your birdhouse to make it last longer.

- To keep plaster from cracking when attaching a picture hook, make an X with two strips of masking tape or transparent tape and drive the nail in where the strips meet.

# Chapter 3

# All Systems Go!

## or A Short History of Our Modern Conveniences

*Remember, nothing that's good works by itself.*
*You've got to make the damn thing work.*
— *THOMAS ALVA EDISON (1847–1931)*

*N*OT ALL MODERN CONVENIENCES ARE QUITE AS MODERN as we may think. Large-scale municipal plumbing, for example, goes back to ancient times. Roman engineers designed and built elaborate aqueducts to carry pure water from mountain rivers to cities and distributed it to public baths and other facilities through a network of lead pipes. (Our word *plumbing* is derived from *plumbum*, the Latin word for "lead.")

We know quite a bit about Roman plumbing, thanks in large part to an engineer by the name of Vitruvius, whose ten-volume reference work on urban planning, architecture, and construction has survived to the present. By and large, the system worked quite well. Unfortunately, though, the Romans never made the connection between their fondness for lead (they also used lead vessels for cooking and corrected sour wine with a sweet extract of condensed grape juice and lead) and the assorted health problems that often plagued them. Modern physicians recognize these problems — including chronic constipation, stomach pain, gout, impotence, and insanity — as major symptoms of what they now call plumbism, or lead poisoning.

With the fall of the Roman Empire in the fifth century (an event that may have been hastened by all that lead), plumbing fell into disuse and remained a lost art throughout the Middle Ages. People went back to hauling water from wells, springs, or rivers. This was inconvenient and often unreliable, but it suited the temper of the times. With the rise of Christianity and its emphasis on spirituality and suffering, anything that tended to increase physical comfort had become a bit suspect.

That emphasis on austerity is best embodied by the dictum of the Franciscan monk William of Ockham (or Occam), who stated, "It is vain to do with more that which can be done with less." Although he was talking about philosophical argument, not plumbing, this was hardly the sort of world-view that would encourage the building of aqueducts to the mountains when it was possible to dip a bucket in a nearby stream.

Only with the Renaissance did creature comfort and running water come back into style. They're still in vogue today, which is why we now enjoy hot tubs, pulsating showerheads, and refrigerator doors that dispense ice water. The ancient Romans might have seen such things as interesting improvements, but they would not have found them altogether new and startling. They would have been utterly astonished, however, by another modern development that most of us take for granted: bright, reliable, inexpensive lighting.

In looking back at some earlier methods of lighting, what's most striking is just how inadequate they were. For most of human history, fires used for heating and cooking were the only source of artificial light, and people simply went to sleep when it got dark. Firelight was later supplemented by oil lamps, which burned vegetable oil, animal fat, or fish oil to produce a dim, smoky, and often malodorous light. Being portable, they were only a slight improvement over firelight.

Candles, which first appeared about 2,000 years ago, were only marginally brighter than oil lamps, but they were far more convenient. Unlike the wax candles we have today, most early candles were made from tallow — essentially solidified animal fat — and tended to melt and grow rancid in storage. The charred wick of a burning candle had to be trimmed periodically, or it would begin to flicker, give off foul-smelling smoke, and eventually go out. The process of trimming the wick was known as snuffing, and if it was done carelessly, the inattentive snuffer would be left in the dark. (Given the fact that the word *snuff* has now become synonymous with *extinguish*, this must have been a common mistake.) Because matches had not yet been invented, this was more than a minor inconvenience. Relighting a candle meant lighting a splinter of wood or a piece of straw in the embers of the fire and applying it to the wick — a ticklish procedure that must have sent many a homeowner to bed in darkness and frustration.

Despite their deficiencies, tallow candles had one important benefit: because tallow is more or less edible, they could — and sometimes did — serve as emergency food during hard times. They were the best thing going until the 17th century, when somewhat brighter, cleaner-burning beeswax candles came into vogue. They were so expensive, however, that only the wealthy could afford them. Until well into the 1800s, ordinary people continued to blunder about in the gloaming with smelly tallow candles or rushlights, crude devices consisting of a rush wick or bundle of vegetable fiber dunked in melted fat.

In 1784, a Swiss physicist named Aimé Argand invented a new type of oil lamp. Its essential feature was a hollow cylindrical wick that admitted air to the center of the flame. While the Argand burner may seem simple in retrospect, it was dramatically brighter and more reliable than anything seen before. For the first time, it was possible to read, write, sew, and perform other everyday tasks comfortably after dark. Moreover, the Argand burner was adaptable to many different fuels, including whale oil, distilled oil of turpentine, colza oil (now called canola oil and used for cooking rather than lighting), and, with its introduction in the late 1850s, kerosene. As a result, it could be used economically almost anywhere, and it rapidly became popular in both Europe and North America.

*Beeswax candles were so expensive that only the wealthy could afford them. Until well into the 1800s, ordinary people continued to blunder about in the gloaming with smelly tallow candles.*

The first gaslights, using gas produced from coal, appeared in the early 1800s. Initially, they were used only for streetlights because the primitive gas burners gave off unpleasant fumes. When they were used indoors, radical measures were sometimes needed to provide adequate ventilation. When gaslights were first used in the British House of Commons, for example, they were installed just above a suspended glass ceiling — a resourceful way of admitting light while excluding fumes.

At about the same time gaslights were becoming popular, an inventive Scotsman named Thomas Drummond devised an entirely new type of light that still survives as a figure of speech. He found that when a flame of oxygen and hydrogen was directed on a cylinder of lime, it would glow with a brilliant white light. Although Drummond's limelight was unsuitable for general lighting, it was widely used as a theatrical spotlight, where it served to illuminate the leading performer on-stage.

By the 1840s or so, improved gaslights were widely used indoors across much of Europe. They were slower to take hold in the United States, however, where they didn't become commonplace until after the Civil War. That was probably because gas, which required centralized production and distribution plants, was practical only in cities, and America was still predominantly rural.

But there may have been a bit of behind-the-scenes chicanery involved as well. The American whaling industry, which supplied the most popular fuel used in conventional oil lamps, enjoyed the support of the federal government, which saw it as an excellent way to ensure a steady supply of trained seamen without the expense of maintaining a peacetime navy. As a result, government lighthouses continued to burn whale oil even after tests had established that gas was brighter, cheaper, and more reliable. That bias may have slowed the acceptance of gaslights for other uses as well.

*The American whaling industry, which supplied the most popular fuel used in conventional oil lamps, enjoyed the support of the federal government, which saw it as an excellent way to ensure a steady supply of trained seamen without the expense of maintaining a peacetime navy.*

Eventually, though, whale oil lost out to gas in the cities and to cheaper kerosene in rural areas. In 1887, gaslights became much brighter and cleaner with the introduction of the incandescent Welsbach mantle, a device still used in gas camping lanterns today. By then, however, gas was already giving way to something even brighter and cleaner: electric light.

The first successful light bulb was developed by the English inventor Joseph Swan in 1878. The following year, Thomas Edison came out with his own version of the incandescent electric light. The two carried on a bitter legal battle for a time but soon joined forces and began to distribute electricity commercially.

Because commercial gas service was already a familiar concept, consumers readily accepted the idea of paying for centrally supplied electricity once they saw how bright and convenient the new lights were. Although there were a few technical problems to work out — Edison's first manufactured bulbs, for example, lasted only about 150 hours before burning out — household electricity was soon a fact of life.

Edison's light bulb quickly became the standard, but his version of the electricity to power it did not. He favored direct current, or DC, while a rival American inventor, George Westinghouse, promoted alternating current, or AC. Although Westinghouse's version had some compelling advantages — AC, for example, could be stepped up to very high voltages, making it possible to transmit power over very long distances, while DC systems required many small, local generating plants — Edison was firmly committed to his approach. The financial stakes were enormous, and the ensuing struggle for market share was hard fought.

A brilliant publicist as well as a brilliant inventor, Edison quickly went on the offensive. He published an 83-page booklet that consisted mostly of accounts of people who had met horrible deaths by coming into contact with his rival's AC apparatus. Never one to let truth stand in the way of a good story, he glossed over the fact that at sufficient voltages, DC could cause electrocution just as readily.

At the time, electricity was so new that the word *electrocute* did not yet exist. Edison proposed a new word, *westinghouse,* to cover death by electricity, and he conducted demonstrations for the press in which he would "westinghouse" stray dogs with AC. His greatest moment came in 1890, when he convinced New York prison authorities, then preparing to execute a man named William Kemmler in the newly devised electric chair, to use AC rather than DC. Ultimately, though, even the inventive Edison was unable to turn the tide, and AC became the accepted standard.

Although electrical service would not reach many rural areas until the 1930s and 1940s, it was widely available in the cities by the turn of the century and soon began creeping out into the suburbs. Electricity became the impetus for other important changes as well. At first it was seen purely in terms of electric lighting (this is why some people still refer to their monthly statement from the power company as the "light bill," even though lighting probably accounts for only a small fraction of the total). But once electricity was available to large numbers of people, it was soon put to work doing other tasks. Enterprising manufacturers began turning out electric irons, stoves, fans, washing machines, and other useful and laborsaving devices. Once all the possible useful devices had been invented, they turned to some that were, well, less useful, such as the electric carving knives that enjoyed a burst of popularity during the early 1960s.

*Once all the possible useful devices had been invented, enterprising manufacturers turned to some that were, well, less useful.*

On balance, though, electricity has made our lives both easier and more productive. We can light up the night as brightly as we care to, making more time for work or play. Electricity cooks our food and distributes heat through our houses even where it doesn't provide heat directly. We no longer have to depend on gravity to move water, as the Romans did, or lug William of Ockham's bucket. We have electric pumps now, and as much water as we need for cooking, drinking, and washing. The nonelectric 19th century — to say nothing of the Middle Ages or ancient Rome — seems almost impossibly remote.

But in something as complex as an electrical supply system, things do go wrong occasionally. (The engineering principle known as Murphy's Law — usually stated as "anything that can possibly go wrong will go wrong" — is often treated as a joke, but it is actually a serious argument in favor of simplicity of design. William of Ockham would have understood it instantly.) When the power goes out, we're effectively plunged back into the first century A.D. Want to warm yourself or cook something? Better build a fire. Need to light up the room? Get a candle — if you happen to have one on hand. It's enough to make you envy the ancient Romans their gravity-fed water, lead pipes and all.

*In the world there is nothing more submissive and weak than water. Yet for attacking that which is hard and strong nothing can surpass it.*

— *LAO-TZU (6TH CENTURY B.C.)*

# How to Avoid a Draining Experience

*BY ROBERT G. WILSON*

All the drains in your house eventually connect into your sewer — the main drain line that runs from your house and leads either to a main sewer system in the street or to your septic tank. For those of you who don't know a lead pipe from a sink trap, this plumbing lesson may have gone far enough. But for anyone who lives in a house with running water, here are some important things to know about your drains.

## At the Kitchen Sink

☛ Let plenty of water run down the drain by keeping the faucet open for up to half a minute each day. (This is also a good practice for all washbasins in your house.) Sink lines commonly get plugged because not enough water is flushed through them, especially after the garbage disposal is used. Run the faucet for about five seconds after you turn off the disposal. This helps flush the line.

☛ Never pour hot grease or oil down the sink drain — whether or not you have a disposal. Animal fat causes other grease, such as soap, to congeal.

☛ About once a month, fill the sink to the top with very hot water. Using a fork or other kitchen utensil (so that you don't scald your hand), remove the sink's plug. As the clean, hot water swirls down through your sink line, it will take much of the grease buildup with it.

## Don't Rely on Chemicals

☛ Drain-cleaning chemicals are dangerous and
unsafe to keep around the house. They can
spill when being used, splash into eyes,
and be found by children.

☛ Many people try chemicals before hir-
ing a drain-cleaning expert because
they want to save
money. Then
they call the
drain cleaner
anyway because
the chemical has-
n't cleared the
drain. Professional drain cleaners are accustomed to working
on chemical-filled lines and know
how to protect themselves. But
even so, it is hazardous to run cables
through a line in which chemicals have
been poured.

☛ Chemicals can solidify in a drain line and aggravate the blockage. For
example, let's say your sink backs up when you turn on the disposal.
You pour a chemical down the drain, hoping to unclog the line. The
stoppage may have been simple, such as a glob of potato peelings the
disposal ignored. If the chemical doesn't eat through the peelings
quickly — and therefore flush on down the drain — the chemical will
sit in your sink line. It will crystallize. There is no way you can easily
clean a sink line after chemicals harden in it. You must call a professional drain cleaner, and he or she may charge more than the minimum fee
because it takes time to clear a line containing crystallized drain cleaner.
Also, the chemical may have become so hard that you have to call a
plumber to replace the entire line.

☛ Picture what happens when a chemical goes down a sink line. First, it
hits the blockage. If it can't immediately loosen it and flush right on
through the line, which it frequently can't, it sits in the line. The first
thing it does is bubble and cook. It becomes hot. When chemicals sit

for some time in a two-inch-diameter line, they can eat through copper, dissolve rubber gaskets, and cause galvanized pipes to corrode — all without eating through the cause of the blockage. And what does the unwary homeowner sometimes do when he or she pours chemicals down a line and the line doesn't immediately open? Pour down more chemicals!

## To Keep a Toilet from Getting Plugged

☛ Don't put anything foreign down the toilet except toilet paper. This includes dental floss, Q-Tips, baby wipes, and any other paper products. Such things cling to the roots in the sewer and cause an immediate blockage. They can become packed in the sewer because they don't flush through to the main line. Then they are expensive to remove, occasionally necessitating sewer repair. If you have a septic system, foreign objects fill your tank and can work their way into your leach field.

## Signs of Big Backups

Don't make the mistake of thinking that a slow drain or drains, such as a washbasin and shower, indicate that the sewer is beginning to plug up or the septic tank needs pumping. Slow drains mean only that the drains need cleaning. (Try a little vinegar and baking soda, followed by boiling water. If that doesn't work, call a professional to do the job.) When your sewer is plugged or your septic tank needs pumping, you'll know it. Here's what will happen:

☛ Water will back up out of your tub drain when you flush your toilet.

☛ When you empty your bathtub, the water will stop flowing and bubble back at you or bubble into the toilet.

☛ When you empty your kitchen sink, the sink water will back up into the toilet.

☛ When you flush your toilet, sewer water will back up through an outside downspout, patio drain, or driveway drain or through the lowest floor drain in your house.

☛ When you run a load of laundry, soapy water will come up into the toilet, shower, or floor drain.

# NECESSARY BUSINESS

For 4,000 years, the place where a person goes to do his or her "business" has never had a straightforward name. The "bath" or "bathroom," after all, is not just for taking a bath, and the "necessary room" is a little oblique. The Israelis went to the "house of honor," the Egyptians to the "house of the morning," the Romans to the "necessarium," and the Tudors to the "privy" or "house of privacy" (or they went to the "Jakes" — Jack's place, because everyone had to go — now known as the "John"). Even sailors, a hardy lot with a reputation for direct language, go to the "head."

Another favorite is the "loo." The word entered the vocabulary in one of several ways. Whenever a Frenchman tossed a load from his window, he first hollered, *"Guardez l'eau"* — "Watch out for the water." It

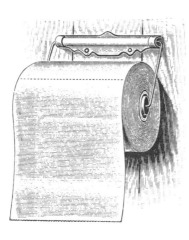

was shortened to *l'eau* and soon became loo. Or, as another story goes, it derived from an abbreviation of a common name for the necessary room, *la chambre sent,* "the smelly room." Apparently to avoid being quite so crude, the people changed the *s* to a *c* — *la chambre cent* — and the common name for the bathroom became "room 100." Soon the numeral 100 became loo, and it stuck.

— *Kenneth Mirvis*

## Faucet Fact

Why is the hot-water faucet on the left and the cold-water faucet on the right? The answer is simple. Until the invention of the water heater, there wasn't such a thing as a hot-water faucet. The knob to turn on the (cold) water was on the right, a convenience for the majority of users (right-handed people). With the introduction of hot-water plumbing, the additional knob was placed on the left.

## Something to Think About

Four trillion gallons of precipitation falls on the United States each day, but only a tenth of it is used, according to *National Geographic*. As water circles from earth to sky, it may be dirtied, but none is lost. The water that John used to baptize Jesus Christ still exists, its billions of molecules now dispersed around the world.

## HOW MUCH WATER DOES A STEAK DINNER COST?

Of all the water used in the United States, about 6 percent is for residential purposes, 14 percent for industrial use, and a whopping 80 percent for agricultural purposes. To put agricultural consumption into perspective, here's what it costs, in terms of gallons of water, to produce a typical American meal.

An 8-ounce baked potato "costs" about 12 gallons of water. Put a single pat of butter on it, and you've "spent" another 100 gallons. If you're having chicken, add 408 gallons, plus 18 gallons for green beans and 6 gallons for a salad, not counting dressing. Dinner rolls at 26 gallons and another 100-gallon pat of butter make for a grand total of 670 gallons of water for the entire meal.

A meal cheaper in price sometimes costs more in water. For instance, a quarter-pound hamburger and bun, fries, and a Coke costs 1,427 gallons of water — and that doesn't count the water used to manufacture and distribute the packaging materials involved.

If you want to go first class and order steak instead of chicken or hamburger, one steak costs about 2,607 gallons of our precious water for every single serving.

# How Much Water Is Used?

### According to the American Water Works

| | GALLONS |
|---|---|
| To brush your teeth (water running) | 1 to 2 |
| To flush a toilet | 5 to 7 |
| To run a dishwasher | 9 to 12 |
| To shave (water running) | 10 to 15 |
| To wash dishes by hand | 20 |
| To take a shower | 15 to 30 |
| By an average person daily | 123 |
| In the average residence during a year | 100,000 |

## H I N T S  &  S U G G E S T I O N S

### In the Bathroom

☞ To prevent bathtub ring, sprinkle some talcum powder in your bath. It will smell good, too!

☞ Keep a sponge mop handy and use it to remove the soap ring that appears in bathtubs (if you forgot the powder). To make the job easier, add a little household ammonia to the sponge.

☞ To prevent a fogged-up mirror, when you run a bath or start a shower, run some cold water first.

☞ To clear a fogged-up mirror (if you forgot to run the cold water first), use a blackboard eraser. This also works for car windshields.

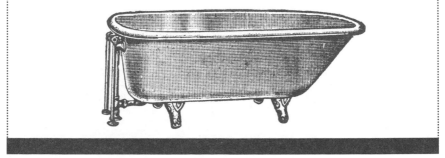

# The Once & Future Fuse Box

*BY STEVE FOWLE*

Like many of my generation, I'm nostalgic for times I can barely recall. I miss cool bottles of milk in the tin box on the doorstep on spring mornings, the tinkling bell of the ice cream truck on hot summer afternoons, and the smell of leaves burning in piles up and down the street in fall. But I'm not completely gaga for the old days. I think some venerable institutions should go the way of smallpox and spats — among them, the fuse box.

My antipathy toward fuse boxes stems from expeditions I made with my father down into our basement to replace blown fuses. The fuse box, as I recall, was located in the farthest, darkest corner of our earthen-floor basement, covered with the dirt of years and the webs of spiders — poisonous, no doubt. As Dad would fiddle and mutter in the dim glow of my flashlight, I could feel black widow spiders climbing over my shirt collar and hear rats sniffing at my sneakers. So when Carl Goodman, local electrician, told me recently that fuse boxes are obsolete, I took the news bravely.

Fuse boxes are the heart of your home electrical system. Apparently, many homes need an electrical heart transplant.

"Until recently," Carl told me, "I didn't recommend replacing fuse boxes unless there was something actually wrong with them. But household-type fuse boxes haven't even been manufactured since the sixties." And the ones still in service are about at the end of their useful lives.

"These boxes have a tar that seals the connections in the back," Carl explained. "Over the years, you'll get heating, corrosion, rust, and/or vibration, and it will start working the box apart. It might last another ten years, but chances are you've gotten your money's worth."

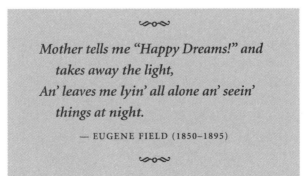

*Mother tells me "Happy Dreams!" and*
*takes away the light,*
*An' leaves me lyin' all alone an' seein'*
*things at night.*

— EUGENE FIELD (1850–1895)

Trying to squeeze another few years out of an old fuse box could be false economy. Nationwide, approximately 40,000 house fires are caused by electrical problems each year. The purpose of fuses (and their modern equivalents, circuit breakers) is to prevent fires and electrocutions by interrupting the flow of electricity to circuits that are drawing more current than they can safely handle. When a fuse blows or a circuit breaker trips, what you *want* is to get the juice flowing again. What you *need* is to know why it stopped and to correct that problem.

## What to Do When the Lights Go Out

The most common problem is overload: too many things plugged into the circuit. The next most likely problem is a short circuit in an appliance or the household wiring.

To find out which event occurred, start by turning off the main power supply at the box. Depending on the age of the installation, this could mean unplugging the "pullouts" (black plastic blocks with large cylindrical cartridge fuses in them), pulling a big handle-type switch on the side of the box, or throwing the main circuit breakers.

Then unplug or turn off everything on the circuit. Look for and replace cracked or melted plugs and worn or frayed wires. Leave everything unplugged.

Install a new fuse or reset the breaker. Wait about a minute. If the fuse blows or the breaker trips off, you know the trouble is in the wiring. If you're not an electrician, call one now.

One by one, test the lamps and appliances as follows: with the fuse out or the breaker off, plug one appliance back in, then screw in the fuse. Repeat the process until a blown fuse tells you that you've found the culprit.

Over the decades, fuse boxes have tended to sprout clusters of smaller boxes all around them, like mushrooms after a rain. This is caused by the continuous stream of new and indispensable electrical widgets, such as curling irons, Lava Lamps, and molten butter dispensers. Existing circuits couldn't handle the increased load, and the original boxes couldn't accommodate new circuits, so more boxes were tacked on. Eventually, the result was a mare's nest of decrepit junk that belongs in the Museum of Obsolete Technology. If that's what you've got, consider replacing your fuse box(es) with a panel of circuit breakers.

Circuit breakers look something like light switches, only they're beefier and mounted horizontally. Unlike fuses, they can be reset. And circuit breakers can't be bypassed by putting a penny in the socket. (All that old trick ever accomplished was to deliver electricity to whatever fire hazard blew the fuse in the first place, causing many a house fire.)

Along with the heart of your electrical service, inspect its arteries — the wiring. If your house was wired to code after 1970 or so, you likely have Romex wire (a plastic-clad, three-conductor cable) and a circuit breaker box. But if your basement or closet hides a Medusa-headed nightmare of frayed wires and rusty fuse boxes, you ought to be concerned.

Old, overburdened, outmoded systems have too few circuits trying to serve too many demands. You need more circuits and a good place to hook them up. Your best bet is to pay a licensed electrician to yank your old fuse box, install a new breaker box, and run new wiring to the heaviest loads: kitchen, bathroom(s), and large appliances. The new circuits will be safe, and the old wiring that remains will be safer because you've reduced the load on it.

If you have any energy and money left after that, you can have the service improved to other parts of the house. Anytime you're renovating or remodeling a room, take a look at how it's wired. There will never be a more convenient or cheaper time to rewire.

Carl Goodman once found a homemade fuse box consisting of a tin candy box with an old knife switch inside, like the ones in the Frankenstein movies. Your electrical system is probably superior to that one, but you won't know until you look. So swallow your fears, gird up your loins, and start down those cellar stairs!

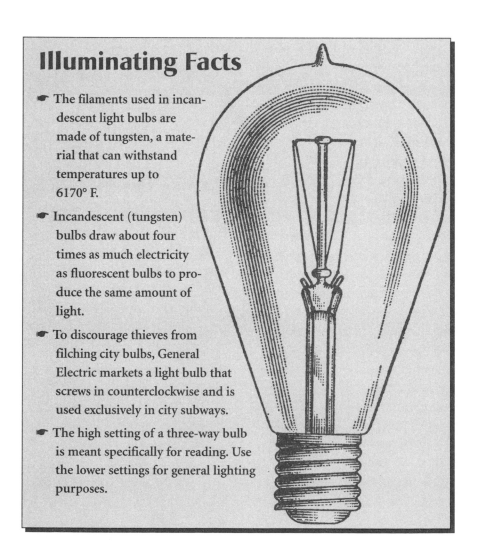

# Illuminating Facts

☞ The filaments used in incandescent light bulbs are made of tungsten, a material that can withstand temperatures up to 6170° F.

☞ Incandescent (tungsten) bulbs draw about four times as much electricity as fluorescent bulbs to produce the same amount of light.

☞ To discourage thieves from filching city bulbs, General Electric markets a light bulb that screws in counterclockwise and is used exclusively in city subways.

☞ The high setting of a three-way bulb is meant specifically for reading. Use the lower settings for general lighting purposes.

# How Much Electricity Is Used?

This table indicates the annual estimated energy consumption for various household electrical products. (Note: One kilowatt equals 1,000 watts; a kilowatt-hour is the work done by one kilowatt in an hour.)

| APPLIANCE | ESTIMATED KILOWATT-HOURS |
|---|---|
| Water heater (standard) | 4,219 |
| Refrigerator (frost-free) | 1,591 to 1,829 |
| Freezer (frost-free) | 1,820 |
| Air conditioner (room) | 1,389 |
| Range (self-cleaning oven) | 1,205 |
| Clothes dryer | 993 |
| Television (color) | 502 |
| Computer | 25 to 400 |
| Dehumidifier | 377 |
| Dishwasher | 165 to 363 |
| Microwave oven | 300 |
| Fan (attic) | 291 |
| Frying pan | 186 |
| Iron | 144 |
| Coffeemaker | 106 |
| Clothes washer | 103 |
| Broiler | 100 |
| Radio | 86 |
| Videocassette recorder (VCR) | 10 to 70 |
| Vacuum cleaner | 46 |
| Fan (circulating) | 43 |
| Garbage disposal | 30 |
| Clock | 17 |
| Blender | 15 |
| Hair dryer | 14 |
| Food mixer | 13 |

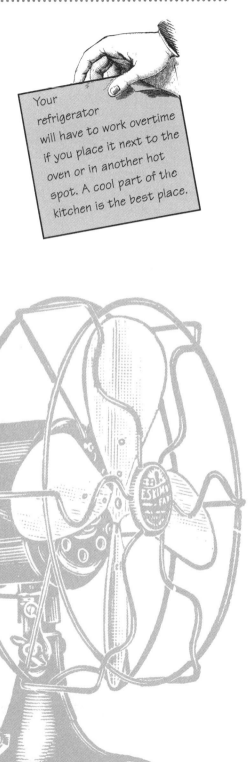

Your refrigerator will have to work overtime if you place it next to the oven or in another hot spot. A cool part of the kitchen is the best place.

# CHECK YOUR LIGHT BULBS IN FALL

The days are becoming perceptibly shorter, and all too soon comes a time when it will be dark at five o'clock. For this reason, the size of the electric light bill will be on the increase, and we will all start and end the day (and even the midday when cloudy) using our artificial lights.

Before long now, you should look over the light bulbs in all the sockets in the house, barns, and outbuildings and be sure they are cleaned of dust and dirt. Between steam, oily and greasy vapors, and dust and dirt, you will be surprised to see how opaque a curtain has collected on them.

Studies of the efficiency of lights show that a loss of 40 percent in lighting efficiency is not uncommon where light bulbs and reflectors are allowed to accumulate dust and dirt. Why pay full price and then get only 60 percent of the value?

Always take the bulbs and reflectors out of or off the sockets before washing, and be sure they are thoroughly dried off before replacing. You'll be surprised how the ones in the barns have needed this treatment and how they respond.

— *The Old Farmer's Almanac,* 1939

## HINTS & SUGGESTIONS

### When the Electricity Goes Out...

☛ If you have trouble making candles fit securely in their holders, try pouring hot water into the candle bowl, let stand to heat the holder, pour out, and put the candle in place immediately. If one application of water does not heat the candlestick sufficiently to secure the candle, repeat the process.

☛ Your candles will burn more slowly if you put them in the freezer before using. Frozen candles also drip and smoke less.

☛ Attach a glow-in-the-dark sticker or piece of luminous tape to your flashlight to make it easier to find when the power goes out. (The flashlight must be out in the open, where the tape can get "charged up.")

# Chapter 4

# Clean &
# Simple,

## or Putting Your Faith in a
## Few Basic Ingredients

*Cleaning anything involves making something else dirty, but
anything can get dirty without something else getting clean.*
— LAURENCE J. PETER (1919–1990)

HOW MANY DIFFERENT CLEANING PRODUCTS DOES YOUR house contain? If you go through the garage, the basement, and your cleaning cupboard, you'll probably turn up dozens of them — an impressive battery of scouring powders, detergents, solvents, polishes, and waxes, to mention just a few. All have their uses, and many of them work very well. Even so, when you contemplate their sheer aggregate mass, it's difficult to avoid the suspicion that maybe — just maybe — there are more of them than you really need.

Not so long ago, there were no specialized cleaning products. A handful of simple household items — soap, white vinegar, baking soda, and table salt, among others

— seemed to take care of most cleaning chores quite well. Although some of the new products on the market really *do* get things cleaner with less effort (or seem to, at least; laundry detergents that contain "brighteners" actually infuse your clothes with fluorescent dyes that glow slightly under ultraviolet light, making them look cleaner than they really are), many perform only slightly better than their generic predecessors.

Of course, that's really not so surprising. Dirt, grease, and grime have not changed over the years. Given the durable, easy-to-clean surfaces found in today's homes — things like laminated countertops, synthetic fabrics, and fiberglass tub-and-shower units — the old-fashioned cleaners actually work better than they ever have.

Something *has* changed, though. It's us. Social change, not chemistry, is responsible for that jumble of plastic bottles in your broom closet. Economics plays a part, too, as do deep-rooted concepts of sex and class. But let's pick an obvious starting point: our age-old dislike of housework.

Before the invention of the washing machine, people went to great lengths to avoid the brutal labor of doing the family laundry by hand. Anyone who could possibly afford to hire the job out did so — including, in many cases, those who earned their own living by doing laundry for others. (That peculiar state of affairs may have given rise to a hypothetical example economists often use to illustrate the limitations of a pure service economy — the imaginary island whose inhabitants make their entire living by taking in one another's laundry.)

Fortunately (or unfortunately, depending on your point of view), there was no shortage of willing hands. Society was far more stratified than it is today, with a small upper class and a very large underclass, whose members had to take what work they could find, at whatever wages they could get.

That state of affairs was particularly pronounced in England, where middle- and upper-class households routinely employed servants in numbers that seem almost unbelievable today. In a book published in 1850, one prominent English architect defined a house as a dwelling that required three or more full-time servants. A dwelling that provided work for just two servants was termed a cottage.

Things were less extreme in the United States, partly because employing servants was seen as undemocratic, but also because the greater range of options available in a large, sparsely settled country reduced the number of people willing to accept such work. Even so, many well-off households employed at least one servant, although the word *servant* tended to raise hackles. European visitors noted that American servants were invariably referred to as "help." (The euphemism *servant* was reserved for southern slaves, who, of course, had no choice of work at all.)

*In some circles, the difficulty of getting good help emerged as a conversational staple. And all but the wealthiest people — however reluctantly — took to doing their own housework.*

Gradually, the overall picture began to change. By the late 1800s, slavery was no more, the American economy was becoming industrialized, and new jobs were opening up in manufacturing. As difficult, unpleasant, and downright dangerous as many of these new jobs undoubtedly were, they were still preferable to working as a servant.

Society adjusted to the change. Architects began designing smaller, more efficient "servantless" houses. In some circles, the difficulty of getting good help emerged as a conversational staple. And all but the wealthiest people — however reluctantly — took to doing their own housework. (OK, let's be honest. As it pertains to housework, the word *people* actually means "women.")

The rise of a manufacturing economy brought other far-reaching changes. Better jobs and higher wages dramatically increased the size of the middle class. This was wonderful in theory, but it had its ironic side. It meant that many recruits to the newly servantless middle class — including some who had once earned meager wages doing laundry, beating carpets, and scrubbing floors in the homes of others — now found themselves working just as hard in their own homes for no wages at all.

As luck would have it, technology soon provided at least partial relief. The development of vacuum cleaners, washing machines, and other laborsaving devices early in the 20th century took much of the hard labor out of cleaning house. Whether such things would have appeared quite so soon if servants were still doing the work is impossible to say. But once the idea of scientific, machine-assisted cleaning had established a foothold, other innovations quickly followed.

*By the 1920s, advertising was already a billion-dollar-a-year business in America, busily pitching everything from soap flakes and breakfast cereals to automobiles. Demand, it turned out, could be manufactured like any other product.*

When washing machines first appeared, for example, laundry soap still came in bars, which had to be grated like cheese before use. Soon, however, soap manufacturers began turning out easy-to-use soap flakes and powders. After World War I, detergents, which outperformed soaps for many tasks, were becoming available as well. (Oddly, however, detergents were not widely used for laundry until after World War II.) So far, so good.

At this point, though, another force, advertising, began to make itself felt — a force fully as powerful and influential as technology itself. By the 1920s, advertising was already a billion-dollar-a-year business in America, busily pitching everything from soap flakes and breakfast cereals to automobiles. Demand, it turned out, could be manufactured like any other product — a discovery that closed the economic circle almost as neatly as that on the faraway "Isle of Laundry."

Like most people, you undoubtedly view advertising

with a healthy skepticism, and you have probably noticed that the smaller the actual differences between products, the harder advertisers work to create imaginary differences. To some extent, that's all to the consumer's benefit. If the only real difference between E-Z Kleen and Redi-Wype window cleaner is in the quality of their advertising, you don't need to agonize over which one to buy.

But it's worth keeping in mind that although advertising offers a range of options for most products, it doesn't offer *all* the options. E-Z Kleen and Redi-Wype are prepared to spend millions trying to win your business, but you'll never see a TV commercial urging you to wash your windows with white vinegar, warm water, and newspaper or to clean your bathtub with baking soda. It's not that those items won't work; it's just that there isn't any money in them for advertisers. But there *is* money in them for you. No matter how often you wash your windows or clean your bathtub, you probably won't save more than a few dollars a year, but that money is better off with you than with the folks at E-Z Kleen or Redi-Wype. They'd just blow it on more advertising.

&infin;o&infin;

*When I was a lad I served a term*
*As office boy to an Attorney's firm.*
*I cleaned the windows and I swept the floor,*
*And I polished up the handle of the big front door.*
*I polished up that handle so carefullee*
*That now I am the ruler of the Queen's Navee!*

— SIR WILLIAM SCHWENCK GILBERT (1836–1911)

&infin;o&infin;

*Always washing, and never getting finished.*
                                    — *THOMAS HARDY (1840–1928)*

# The Virtues of Vinegar, Lemons & Salt

*The Old Farmer's Almanac* has long been a proponent of the cleaning power of vinegar, lemons, and salt (and other equally down-to-earth ingredients). Following is a compilation of years of Almanac cleaning advice.

## IN THE KITCHEN

### APPLIANCES

*Dishwasher*
- ☛ To help keep the drain line clean and sweet smelling, add ½ cup white vinegar to the rinse cycle.
- ☛ Fresh lemon juice will remove soap film from the interior.

*Garbage Disposal*
- ☛ If the rubber shield smells after much use, soak it in a pan of white vinegar.
- ☛ Toss used lemons into your garbage disposal to help keep it clean and fresh smelling.

*Humidifier*
- ☛ To clean the filter, remove it and soak it in a pan of white vinegar until all the sediment is off. Then wash in dishwashing detergent and water.

*Stove*
- ☛ Filmy dirt and grease on the stovetop will come clean with white vinegar.
- ☛ To prevent grease buildup, dampen a rag with a solution of white vinegar and water and wipe out the interior of the oven.
- ☛ Oven spills will stop smoking if you sprinkle them with salt. Wipe with a damp cloth after the oven cools.
- ☛ If something in the oven catches on fire, salt or baking soda will help smother the flames.

☞ A mixture of salt and cinnamon makes a good oven freshener. Sprinkle spills while the oven is still warm to take away the burned smell.

### Refrigerator

☞ Half a lemon placed on a shelf will absorb odors.

☞ Salt and baking soda in water will clean and sweeten the inside of your refrigerator.

## METALS

☞ **Chrome:** Clean off soap and stains with a mixture of 1 teaspoon salt and 2 tablespoons white vinegar. To shine chrome and remove spots, rub with a piece of lemon rind, then wash and dry with a soft cloth.

☞ **Chrome and Stainless Steel:** Shine with a cloth sprinkled generously with flour. Rub well, then dust off gently with another cloth.

☞ **Stainless Steel:** Remove white hard-water stains by rubbing with white vinegar.

☞ **Brass, Copper, and Bronze:** Make a thick paste of salt, white vinegar, and flour. Rub it on the metal, then wash, rinse, and wipe dry.

☞ **Copper and Brass:** Rub with lemon juice or, for heavy corrosion, a paste of lemon juice and salt. Wash, rinse, and wipe dry.

☞ **Copper:** Dip sorrel leaves in hot water and rub the metal to a rich shine.

## WORKING WITH THE WEATHER

### Heavy-Duty Cleaning

Save chores such as scouring the oven for a day with a brisk breeze, since many cleaning products give off potentially harmful fumes. Whether you're using a commercial cleaner or ammonia or simply turning on your oven for its self-cleaning operation, for good ventilation open the windows on a dry day when the air is moving. Open both a kitchen window and one on the opposite side of the house to get a cross draft. Chlorine bleach and other solutions for cleaning bathroom tiles also should be used only with cross ventilation. As a general rule, unless it's plain soap, if you can smell it and it is used for cleaning, get it out of the air as quickly as possible. A heavy, humid day, even with the help of a window fan, is not the right time.

*—Barbara Radcliffe Rogers*

- **Silver:** To ease polishing, rub with salt before washing and polishing.
- **Silverware:** To remove stains, place silverware in a pan and cover with sour milk. Let stand overnight. In the morning, rinse with cold water, then hot water.
- **Aluminum Utensils:** When discolored, boil in lemon juice or sliced lemon and water to renew the shine. Or clean with a cloth dipped in lemon juice, then rinse with warm water.

- **Aluminum Pans:** Remove dark stains by filling the pan with water, adding 1 tablespoon white vinegar for each quart of water, and boiling for ten minutes.
- **Sooty Pans:** Before using a pan for outdoor cooking, coat the bottom with soap. The soot that accumulates during cooking will wash off easily with the soap.
- **Greasy Pans:** Sprinkle with salt, then wipe with a paper towel.
- **Pans with Burned-On Food:** Fill with cold water, add 2 to 3 tablespoons salt, and let stand overnight. In the morning, bring the water slowly to a boil, and your pan will be clean.

### DISHES & GLASSWARE

- To remove chalky deposits, put dishes and glassware in the dishwasher. Place a cup filled with white vinegar on the bottom rack. Run the dishwasher for five minutes, stop the machine, and empty the cup (now full of water). Refill with vinegar. Complete the cycle. Follow with another complete cycle using dishwasher detergent.

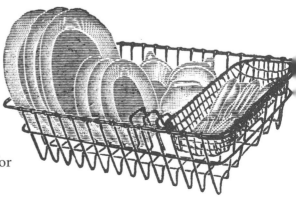

- To remove cloudy mineral deposits from drinking glasses, put a tablespoon of lemon juice in each glass and fill with hot water. Let stand for several hours, then wash.

☛ To remove mineral deposits from baby bottles, add lemon juice to the water when boiling the bottles.

☛ Let discolored or stained bottles, jars, and vases stand for some time in a solution of salt and white vinegar. Shake well and rinse.

☛ Rub glass decanters with a cut lemon or soak in lemon juice and water. Dry with a lint-free cloth. To renew the sparkle and brightness inside, add a little water and a small piece of freshly cut lemon and shake well.

☛ Use lemon juice and salt to return the luster to china.

☛ To remove tea stains, scrub teacups and teapots vigorously with salt, then wash and dry.

## MISCELLANEOUS

☛ **Countertops:** Laminated counters and tabletops can be cleaned by rubbing with a soft cloth soaked in white vinegar. This also makes them shine. To remove stains without scratching, make a paste of baking soda and water. Apply it to the stain, let sit for a minute or two, and rub to remove.

☛ **Drip Coffeemakers:** To clean, fill the reservoir with white vinegar and run through a brewing cycle.

☛ **Pastry Boards and Rolling Pins:** Bleach by occasionally rubbing with a cut lemon.

☛ **Closed Containers:** Use salt to deodorize Thermoses and other closed containers.

☛ **Sponges:** Soak in cold salt water to refresh.

# IN THE BATHROOM

## TUBS, BOWLS & SINKS

☞ Rub tubs and sinks with half a lemon dipped in borax to renew the sparkle.

☞ Clean discolored white enamel with a cloth saturated with salt and turpentine.

☞ To remove bathtub and sink film, wipe with white vinegar, then baking soda. Rinse with water.

☞ Clean and deodorize the toilet bowl by pouring white vinegar into it. Let stand for five minutes, then flush. Spray stubborn stains with vinegar, then scrub vigorously.

## FAUCETS

☞ Remove hard white calcium deposits by soaking toilet tissue with white vinegar and placing it around the stains. Leave tissue in place for an hour or two.

☞ To shine and remove spots, rub faucets with a piece of lemon rind, then wash and dry with a soft cloth.

☞ To renew the shine, sprinkle a cloth generously with flour, then rub faucets well. Dust off gently with a clean cloth.

## MISCELLANEOUS

☞ **Tiles:** Wipe with a cloth soaked in lemon juice, then polish with a chamois cloth.

☞ **Showerhead:** To unclog, soak in diluted white vinegar overnight. Or put some vinegar in a plastic bag, tie it around the showerhead, and leave on overnight.

☞ **Mirror:** To prevent the bathroom mirror from steaming up, rub it with soap and then polish.

☞ **Plastic Shower Curtain:** Wash the curtain in the machine with bath towels. Add 1 cup white vinegar to the rinse cycle. Briefly tumble dry. For a quick cleanup, use a sponge dampened with vinegar. (Don't bother to take the curtain down.)

# FLOORS, WALLS & FURNISHINGS

## FLOORS

### No-Wax Vinyl Flooring

☛ To clean and shine, add ½ cup white vinegar to ½ gallon warm water.

### Carpets

☛ To bring out the color in rugs and carpets, brush them with a mixture of 1 cup white vinegar and 1 gallon water. Or wipe them vigorously with a damp cloth soaked in a strong salt solution.

☛ Animal urine stains and odors can usually be vanquished by using a mixture of equal parts white vinegar and water. Sponge it into the carpet and then blot it up with thick towels. If the stain is near the wall, also wash the wall (about 18 inches up) with the mixture, as the culprit may have been a male cat.

☛ To make your own carpet (and upholstery) shampoo, combine 1 quart water, ¼ cup mild powdered detergent, and 1 tablespoon white vinegar. Using an eggbeater, whip into a stiff foam. Apply to the fabric with a soft brush, sponge, or terry cloth, rubbing gently and using even pressure to prevent streaking. Scrape away soiled foam with a dull knife. Wipe off residue with a damp cloth or sponge.

☛ To clean up coffee spills, blot up excess coffee, then rub the stain with a solution of water, mild powdered detergent, and white vinegar (see previous tip).

☛ Remove greasy spills by sponging with a solution of four parts alcohol and one part salt.

### Wood & Tile Floors

☛ To whiten an unpainted wood floor, sprinkle freely with clean white sand. Leave the sand on the floor for a few days. In the process of walking to and fro, the family will keep the boards scoured to a snowy white. (To make floor sand, purchase marble clippings. In an old iron kettle, heat until red. When cold, pulverize.)

☛ Wash a wood or tile floor with an orange cut in half. Put one half in each hand, get down on your knees, and work in circles to remove grease and dirt. Rinse with a damp rag.

## WALLS

☛ **Wood Paneling:** Combine 1 quart warm water, ¼ cup white vinegar, and 2 tablespoons olive oil. Dampen a soft cloth with this solution and wipe the paneling, then wipe with a dry cloth.

☛ **Glossy Wall Finish:** To give whitewashed walls a glossy finish, dissolve 1 pound soap powder in 1 gallon hot water and add to 5 gallons whitewash.

☛ **Painted and Varnished Surfaces:** To clean, use a solution of 1 gallon warm water, 1 cup ammonia, ½ cup white vinegar, and ¼ cup baking soda. There is no need to rinse or dry the surface. The solution will not dull the finish.

☛ **Woodwork:** Remove fingerprints by rubbing a slice of potato over the stain. After general cleaning, rinse with the juice of 1 lemon diluted in 1 quart water to maintain the woodwork's shine.

☛ **Windows and Mirrors:** Add 2 tablespoons white vinegar to 1 cup water and put in a spray bottle. Spray the window or mirror lightly and wipe with crumpled newspaper. Avoid the edges of mirrors, as moisture will spoil the silver on the back.

☛ **Fireplace Bricks:** Brush with white vinegar.

## WORKING WITH THE WEATHER

### *Washing Windows*

When the sun is shining brightly, you may notice that your windows need washing, but that's not the best time to do them. Instead, choose an overcast, fairly warm day without a breeze. Windows washed in the sunlight or on a windy day will streak much more readily than those washed on a cloudy day, as the latter will dry more slowly. You can wipe away the streaks as you see them, before they dry into ones that will need to be removed with a wet cloth.

You don't want to wash windows on a really cold day either. Very cold glass also streaks badly, and you'll lose heat from the house as you open and close the windows to wash them. — *Barbara Radcliffe Rogers*

## FURNISHINGS

### Wood

☞ Clean discolored or dirty wood with a mixture of equal parts turpentine, white vinegar, and mineral oil. Shake well before and during use. Apply with a soft cloth and rub vigorously.

☞ Wake up dull-looking wood furniture by polishing with a piece of salt pork.

☞ For mahogany furniture, mix 3 tablespoons white vinegar with 1 quart water. Dip a sponge in this solution, wring out well, and polish the furniture.

☞ To dust corners and carvings on furniture, slip an old sock over one hand and use it as a dust cloth.

☞ To remove scratches, combine equal parts lemon juice and salad oil. Apply with a soft cloth and rub until scratches disappear.

☞ White rings from wet glasses may be removed with a mixture of equal parts olive oil and white vinegar. Rub with the grain of the wood. Let stand for an hour or two, then wipe off and apply a coat of polish. Or cover the ring with petroleum jelly, let stand for 24 hours, and wipe off.

### Wicker

☞ Scrub with a stiff brush that has been moistened with warm salt water. Salt also keeps wicker from yellowing.

☞ Vacuum your wicker furniture often and use furniture polish to enhance stained or natural pieces.

### Marble

☞ To clean white marble, rub with half a lemon or a paste made of salt and lemon juice. Wipe with a clean, wet cloth.

☞ To polish marble, use chalk moistened with water.

### Ivory

☞ To whiten ivory piano keys or utensil handles, rub with half a lemon dipped in salt.

### Leather

☞ To clean leather picture frames, bookbindings, and furniture, combine equal parts lemon juice and warm water. Apply to the leather, then wipe clean with a dry cloth.

# LAUNDRY & STAIN REMOVAL

## APPLIANCES

☞ To clean out the hoses and deodorize the tub of your washing machine, fill the machine with water and add 1 quart white vinegar. Run through a complete cycle.

☞ To clean your steam iron, fill the tank with white vinegar and let stand overnight. Rinse thoroughly with warm water. (Be sure to keep the cord dry.)

☞ If your iron is leaving sticky black spots on your clothes, sprinkle a little salt on a piece of paper and run the hot iron over it. The crud will fall right off.

## GENERAL CLEANING

☞ **Silk:** Add ½ cup mild detergent and 2 tablespoons white vinegar to 2 quarts very cold water. Dunk silks up and down in the mixture, but do not soak. Rinse. Roll in a heavy towel and iron while still damp. If you are uncertain about washability, test the item by dipping an inconspicuous part in the solution.

☞ **Linen, Wool, and Silk:** To prevent yellowing, especially of garments and blankets to be stored, add ½ cup white vinegar to the rinse water.

☞ **Leather:** Clean with a mixture of 1 cup boiled linseed oil and 1 cup white vinegar.

- **Slickers and Such:** When washing foul-weather gear or shower curtains, put a couple of towels in the same load. The towels' rough surfaces will rub against the slick ones to help clean them, and they will absorb excess water in the rinse cycle.
- **Nylon Curtains:** Whiten nylon curtains by adding Epsom salts to the rinse water.
- **Baby Clothes and Diapers:** Add 1 cup white vinegar to each load during the rinse cycle. Vinegar breaks down uric acid and soapy residue, leaving clothes soft and fresh.
- **Colored Fabrics:** Salt added to the wash water prevents colored fabrics from running.
- **Smoky Clothes:** Fill the bathtub with hot water and add 1 cup white vinegar. Hang clothes over the steaming water.
- **Smelly Sneakers:** Sprinkle salt in sneakers or other canvas shoes to deodorize.
- **Static Guard:** When washing plastic curtains, add 1 tablespoon white vinegar to each gallon of rinse water. Plastic upholstery also may be wiped clean with a cloth dampened with a solution of water and vinegar. Vinegar cuts down on the attraction of dust.
- **Starch Booster:** If you hang your clothes outside to dry, add salt to the starch water to keep clothes starched while the wind whips them dry.
- **Winterproofed Clothespins:** Clothespins soaked in a strong brine won't freeze to the line in winter. One treatment will last the season.

## STAINS

- **Oily Stains:** Make a paste of granulated sugar and water. Rub it into the stain and let it set before washing.
- **Nonoily Stains:** Make a solution of 1 pint lukewarm water, 1 teaspoon liquid detergent, and 1 teaspoon white vinegar. Apply to the stain with a soft brush or towel, rub gently, and rinse with a towel dampened with water. Blot dry and repeat until the stain is gone. Dry quickly using a fan or hair dryer.
- **Ink:** Saturate with hair spray, allow to dry, then brush lightly with a solution of equal parts white vinegar and water. Or "if [the spot] has

dried in, rub table salt upon it, and drop lemon juice upon the salt. White soap diluted with vinegar is likewise a good thing" (Lydia Maria Child, *The American Frugal Housewife*, 1833).

☛ **Salt and Water:** White vinegar takes salt and water stains off leather boots and shoes. Wipe over the stained area only, then polish.

☛ **Hair Dye:** Wash fabrics stained with hair dye in detergent and white vinegar. Then bleach with hydrogen peroxide and relaunder.

☛ **Lipstick:** Use full-strength lemon juice to remove lipstick from white washable fabrics. Dilute lemon juice in water for colored fabrics.

☛ **Rust:** Make a paste of lemon juice and salt and apply to the stain. Place the fabric in the sun or hold over steam until the stain disappears.

☛ **Mildew:** Try laundering with bleach and drying in the sun. If the stain remains, rub with salt, then lemon juice. Place in the sun.

☛ **Perspiration:** Add ¼ cup salt to 1 quart hot water and sponge the fabric with the solution until the stain disappears. Or rub shampoo (which is formulated to remove body oils) into the stain.

☛ **Wine and Fruit Juice:** Make a paste of lemon juice and salt, apply to the stain, and let sit for 30 minutes. Rinse, then wash in soapy water. If wine or fruit juice stains your tablecloth, cover at once with salt, then rinse later with cool water.

☛ **Handkerchief Stains:** Stubborn handkerchief stains come clean if soaked for 30 minutes in salt water before washing in hot water.

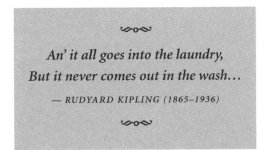

∽∘∾

*An' it all goes into the laundry,*
*But it never comes out in the wash...*

— *RUDYARD KIPLING (1865–1936)*

∽∘∾

# From Carpet Beaters
# to Suction Sweepers
*BY JIM COLLINS*

Once upon a time, say around 1890, deciding how to clean your carpets was a simple matter. Either you were old-fashioned and waited until spring, when you brought them outside to drape over ropes and fences and beat the dust out of them, or you bought a Bissell carpet sweeper and did the dirty work indoors. That mechanical sweeper — whose brushes stirred dirt up into a collecting box — was the first sweeping advancement in hundreds of years, and it revolutionized the chore. Queen Victoria ordered some of these sweepers for Buckingham Palace; so did Turkish sultans and Arabian sheiks for their Oriental carpets. In the age of Louis Pasteur and Florence Nightingale and a growing international obsession with hygiene, the Bissell was all the rage.

By 1920, the cleaning decision had become only slightly more complicated. Improvements had been made on the 1901 "suction cleaner" patented by English inventor H. Cecil Booth. No longer were the units as large as refrigerators, nor did they need two people to operate them. These new portable vacuum cleaners left the Bissell in the dust. Two American companies had a corner on the market. For the most part, you went with a Hoover or a Regina, or you went without.

The Hoover, in particular, was a classic American success story. James Murray Spangler, a janitor from Ohio with a severe allergy to dust, had become desperate. He could barely tolerate the coughing and sneezing fits brought on by the dust from the mechanical sweeper he used, yet he couldn't afford to quit his job. Instead, he toyed with an electric fan, a soapbox sealed with masking tape, and a pillowcase for a dust bag, creating a contraption that looked like a combination bagpipe and breadbox. It worked. He scraped together some money to start the Electric Suction Sweeper Company, sold a machine to a suitably impressed customer named Susan Hoover, and then sold the manufacturing rights to her husband, William, a prosperous Ohio businessman. While Spangler went on to become Hoover's superintendent of production, "Hoover" went on to become a household name synonymous with 20th-century housecleaning.

## WHERE DOES DUST COME FROM?

As we attack it with a vengeance (or a mild swipe now and then), it's tempting to wonder, Where does dust come from? A lot of it comes from people. Although we may not see it, our shoes bring in tiny dirt particles that become airborne as we travel from room to room. Our bodies also produce dust — almost a pound per person per year — in the form of dead skin (which in turn supports microscopic dust mites). And cigarette smoke and cooking odors are actually made up of tiny particles that eventually settle as dust.

What's a housekeeper to do? Focus your attention on places that distribute the most dust, such as radiators, heat registers, and wood-burning stoves, and vacuum them frequently. Set out a cocoa-fiber doormat to scrub dirt from the soles of shoes and boots. Take your shoes off at the door and ask guests to do the same. Keep slippers for your family under a bench where all can sit to take off outdoor shoes. And if you're in the market for a new vacuum cleaner, invest in one that comes with an air filter to trap dust particles, not just send them from room to room.

— *Jon Vara*

## WORKING WITH THE WEATHER

### Dusting

What can you do best on a dull, rainy, still day? Dust. The minute particles that usually float about in the air will be more settled, and more of them will be captured on your dust cloth. It's also a good time to do tasks that create dust, such as cleaning the ashes out of the fireplace or wood stove or emptying the vacuum cleaner. Dust will settle closer to its source and not spread so easily throughout the house. — *Barbara Radcliffe Rogers*

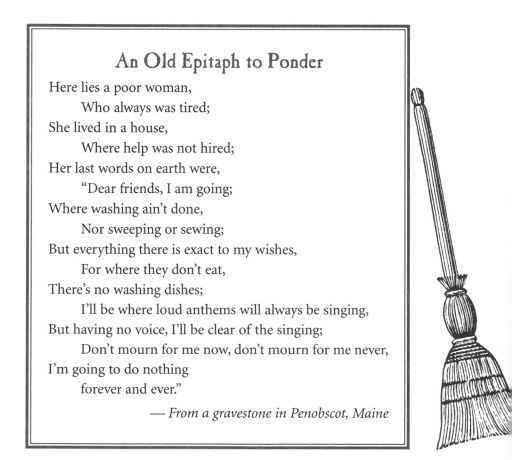

## An Old Epitaph to Ponder

Here lies a poor woman,
    Who always was tired;
She lived in a house,
    Where help was not hired;
Her last words on earth were,
    "Dear friends, I am going;
Where washing ain't done,
    Nor sweeping or sewing;
But everything there is exact to my wishes,
    For where they don't eat,
There's no washing dishes;
    I'll be where loud anthems will always be singing,
But having no voice, I'll be clear of the singing;
    Don't mourn for me now, don't mourn for me never,
I'm going to do nothing
    forever and ever."

— *From a gravestone in Penobscot, Maine*

# Chapter 5

# Making a House a Home,

## or Sharing the Place You Love with the Ones You Love

*Not chaos-like together crush'd and bruis'd,*
*But, as the world, harmoniously confus'd.*
*Where order in variety we see,*
*And where, though all things differ, we agree.*

—*ALEXANDER POPE (1688–1744)*

HUMAN BEINGS ARE NATURALLY GREGARIOUS. THAT'S why we join social clubs, throw Tupperware parties, and go to class reunions. It's why few young people aspire to grow up and become hermits, and why married couples have a habit of subtly — or not so subtly — trying to nudge single friends into getting married.

But in spite of our need for company — or maybe because of it — we also cherish solitude. When we describe someone as independent or self-sufficient, we invariably mean it as a compliment. And even the most sociable person needs to spend some time alone every now and then.

In other words, we're inconsistent. That's not particularly surprising — in fact, you could argue that human behavior is essentially a mass of inconsistencies — but what *is* surprising is how adept we are at juggling such conflicts. Somehow or other, we manage to accommodate our own needs and desires to those of our coworkers, friends, and family members so that most of us, most of the time, are reasonably happy.

You could say that we have an instinct for getting along with others. Humans have lived together in small bands since they first came down from the trees and learned to walk upright. It's reasonable to suppose that the sense of security associated with being part of such a group has been passed down to us. And although we no longer have to fear voracious saber-toothed tigers, the instinct to form groups may still pay real dividends: modern population studies consistently show that married people live significantly longer, on average, than those who remain single.

But instinct is only part of the picture. Most of the important choices we make in life — and most of the unimportant ones, too — call for conscious decisions. Instinct probably played a part in determining whom you considered as a potential spouse, but your final choice was grounded in a conscious, realistic evaluation of your prospective partner's personal attributes and how they might complement (or perhaps clash with) your own. Let's hope so anyway. When reason and instinct are in agreement, happi-

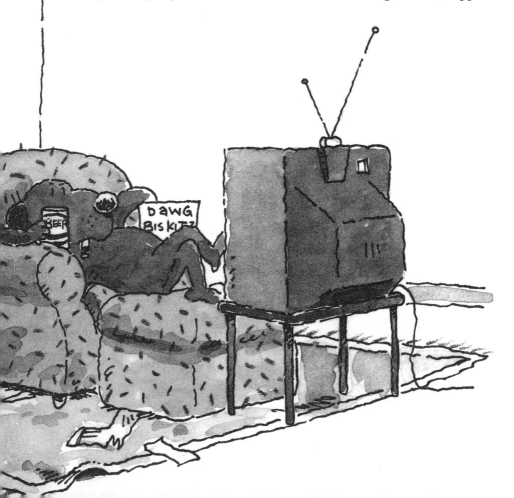

ness often follows. When they disagree, all sorts of household problems are likely to crop up.

Take something as simple as selecting a family pet. In such cases, instinct always takes the same position: it wants a big dog, which it believes will be useful for running down game, providing protection from wolves and other predators, and serving as a warm blanket on chilly nights in the cave.

*When reason and instinct are in agreement, happiness often follows. When they disagree, all sorts of household problems are likely to crop up.*

At this point, reason has several choices. It can put its foot down, insist that such things just aren't important in late-20th-century New Jersey, and hold out for a parakeet or some tropical fish. Instinct may sulk about this for a while, but it will soon get over it. Or reason can try striking a bargain. It can come back with an offer of a small or midsize dog, on the condition that it be well trained and cared for. The one thing reason should never do in such cases is to give instinct the big dog and simply hope for the best. Unfortunately, that's often what happens, and the usual result is a demoralizing sequence of events that usually looks something like this:

**Step 1.** In anticipation of mutually rewarding long-term relationship, well-meaning person acquires puppy.

**Step 2.** After brief period of extreme cuteness, young dog develops one or more bad habits (biting, barking, chasing deer, burying bones in upholstered furniture). Owner hopes that such problems will go away as dog matures.

**Step 3.** Problems persist. Desultory effort to reform dog, either by purchasing dog-training handbook or enrolling dog in obedience school.

**Step 4.** Owner convinces self that dog's behavior is improving slightly, even as it gradually worsens.

**Step 5.** Reluctant admission that training has not been

entirely successful. Repetition of steps 3 and 4.

**Step 6.** Repetition of step 5.

**Step 7.** Dog conceded to be a full-fledged disaster. Mailman does not like dog. Neighbors do not like dog. Owner does not like dog. Owner, however, blames self for not addressing problems early and/or forcefully enough. Years of doubt and exasperation ensue.

**Step 8.** With dog now well into middle age, decision made to sit tight and wait things out. Dog slows down with age, and its capacity to cause trouble gradually diminishes.

**Step 9.** As hoped in step 2, dog has outgrown most early problems. Too weak to bite or chase cars, aged animal becomes object of pity. Early transgressions are forgiven.

**Step 10.** Old Barky limps off to that Great Water Dish in the Sky. General lamentation; agreement that although he had his faults, he was a good dog at heart. Passage of decent interval followed by repetition of step 1.

This is not to suggest that all dogs are bad. Still, the frequency with which bad dogs are encountered — and even dog lovers will admit that they are far from rare — says something about our willingness to make long-term decisions without benefit of conscious thought. We do it all the time. On some level, the workaholic executive who lets his work keep him from spending time with his family probably believes that he's busy stockpiling edible roots for the winter.

There's no way to banish instinct from your life, nor is there any need to. It often provides useful hunches about things and will insist on making itself heard. But don't believe everything it tells you. Instinct tends to take a short-term view of things, probably because it thinks we're still living in caves, when the average human life expectancy was somewhere in the neighborhood of 25 years.

Moreover, because instinct is so different from reason, it

never has second thoughts. In its own eyes, it is never wrong. That may be why ill-advised actions taken at the prodding of instinct tend to go uncorrected for a long time, even after it becomes obvious that things aren't working out as expected.

The solution, quite simply, is to rely on reason more. It's tempting to believe that living together in harmony is just a matter of doing what comes naturally, but that's the voice of instinct again. Get in the habit of thinking about the effects your actions have on those you love. Talk. Listen. Learn to recognize problems and look for solutions.

Sure, all this takes some effort. But it's better than seeing your home life gradually go to the dogs.

*It isn't that we talk so much, —*
*    Sometimes the evening through*
*You do not say a word to me,*
*    I do not talk to you.*
*You sit beside your reading lamp,*
*    I like my easy chair,*
*And it is joy enough for me*
*    To know that you are there.*

— ANNE CAMPBELL (1888–?)

*Family jokes, though rightly cursed by strangers, are the bond that keeps most families alive.*

— *STELLA BENSON (1892–1933)*

## MARITAL ADVICE
### FROM *THE OLD FARMER'S ALMANAC*

☞ He who consults his spouse will have a good counselor. I have heard our minister say, "Women's instincts are often truer than man's reason." They jump at a thing at once and are wise offhand. Say what you will of your wife's advice, it's likely you'll be sorry you did not take it. — *1889*

☞ It is just as much the husband's business "to make the home the brightest and most alluring haven of rest and peace upon all the earth" as it is the wife's. The idea that a mother who has been "worked and worried to death" all day by the cares and annoyances of a household, perhaps with a sick child to nurse and in feeble health at that, should have to go beyond her powers of endurance in order to "make home attractive" to some great lubber of a husband, with muscles of an ox, the health of a whale, and the digestion of an ostrich, is utterly absurd and inhuman. — *1890*

☞ A shrewd old gentleman once said to his daughter, "Be sure, my dear, you never marry a poor man, but remember the poorest man in the world is one that has money, and nothing else." — *1894*

☞ A wife's wages are love, thoughtful attentions, little courtesies. Don't skimp on her pay. — *1921*

☞ If you are having frequent marital squabbles, you could go to see a therapist, but what might really help even more is to install a second bathroom in your house. One study found that couples with more than one bathroom, whether they had children or not, were less stressed and more content than those in single-bathroom homes. — *1992*

# TUGGING AT THE HEART OF IT

In 1770, Samuel Forbes was building a house on the Blackberry River in Canaan, Connecticut. During that time, he fell in love with a young woman named Lucy Peirce. It was a good match, for she equaled him in physique and strength of will. She also loved him. One night the two rode off to New York State — as the story goes, on the same unhappy horse — and were married.

When they arrived back home in Connecticut, Samuel took a long rope and threw one end over the barn. "Now, my sweet," he reportedly said to his bride, "do you draw down on your end and I will draw on mine, and whichever draws the other over the roof is to rule this roost."

They both tugged hard. Nothing happened.

"Now, my sweet," Samuel called, "do you come around on this side, and let us draw together."

Lucy complied. Together they pulled the rope over the barn.

"Let that be the way this house will be run," declared Samuel. And apparently it was.

— *Christine Schultz*

---

*One should never know too
precisely whom one has married.*

— FRIEDRICH WILHELM NIETZSCHE
(1844–1900)

# Rearing Young Children

Give children simple jobs that they can do to help in the home — duties that, as their shoulders broaden, may become real. "May I help, Mother?" Often it takes time and trouble to say "Yes," because we could do it so much better and more quickly. But if we would not keep our children dependent upon us, we must deliberately stand back and efface ourselves in order to give them a chance to decide small points when they are young, so that they may carry large responsibilities later. As Dorothy Canfield Fisher says, a "mother is not a person to lean upon, but a person to make leaning unnecessary!"

Be as versatile as you can in suggestions about what he may do — but have few "don'ts." Interest him in doing of constructive things, but do not emphasize it when you must say no. Divest the negative attitude of your own emotion. If you work yourself up about it, the edge will show in your voice, and you will have made an unfortunate impression. This is losing ground instead of gaining. Think before you say no, and remember that, living so entirely in the present, each event, trivial to you, is of exaggerated importance to the child. Say no only when necessary, but when you must say it, mean it. Put yourself in the place of the child, shut your eyes, and, limiting yourself to this knowledge and experience, imagine what he thinks of you and your actions. This should be a revealing experience.

Remember to show your satisfaction when your child tries to do the right thing, and to pay little attention to his failures.

— *The Old Farmer's Almanac,* 1937

# Good Old Games

*BY GLENN R. WILLISTON*

Perhaps one of the most fascinating aspects of any civilization is the number and variety of children's games and pastimes. An almost uncanny similarity exists between societies in the area of children's games. Top spinning, for example, is as old as Rome, and even older records show the popularity of tops in the ancient Orient.

Today's child is often torn between the pleasures derived from a game he or she knows well and the wonder of a new, highly advertised toy. Games and toys come in all sorts of packaging for eye appeal, but often that appeal is short-lived. When the batteries wear out, Baby-Do-Everything does nothing; when the bits of cardboard and plastic for the TV game are lost, the box is put aside; and when the magic, secret jet fuel runs out, the rocket is placed upon a shelf. At this point, the child turns to the age-old pastimes that have given countless generations endless joy.

## Hopscotch

Generations of American children have made famous games such as the ever-popular hopscotch. In colonial times, "scotch-hoppers," as it was called, was played according to the same rules as it is today. In a centuries-old children's book called *Youthful Recreations,* scotch-hoppers is vaguely described as an "exercise frequently practiced by the Greek and Spartan women."

## Tag

The children's game with the greatest number of variations appears to be tag, and many varieties of the game have come down to us from our colonial ancestors. When the streets of Boston and Concord were nothing but dirt lanes and cowpaths, children of all ages shouted with excitement while engaging in the merriment of tell tag, stone tag, and wood tag.

## Cat's Cradle

One of the most historic games of all — one that gave early New England children many hours of pleasure — is what has been called cat's cradle or cratch cradle. Although most people today know it as cat's cradle, it appears that cratch cradle is the "correct" name of much older origin and that cat's cradle is simply a mispronunciation with the wrong association. (A cratch was a grated crib or manger related particularly to the story of the birth of Christ.) By either name, the procedure is the same: a continuous piece of twine or string is looped over the extended fingers of both hands in a symmetrical pattern. A second person must remove the string, without losing the loops, to create a different pattern or figure.

## Kite Flying

Traditionally in the country, the first mild April breezes lift tugging kites from the hands of excited children. Perhaps kite designs have changed a bit (few are homemade today), but youngsters still look forward to reeling out the taut line and feeling the lifelike tug of a kite at the other end.

## Singing

Historic singing games and rounds sound today as they did in generations past, for each generation has passed the words and music on to the next. Strains of "London Bridge Is Falling Down" are sung by schoolchildren in all corners of the world.

Each year, from Maine to Florida, the game-playing cycle continues. The "right" time comes for marbles and yo-yos. Then come tops, then kites, for the saying goes "Top time's gone, kite time's come, April Fools' Day will soon be here." In Boston and Providence, ball time is always the first Thursday in April. And whistle-making time comes at the moment when whistle wood is "just right." For countless generations, children have shared the joys of the same games at the same times of year.

# The Family Medicine Chest

*M*ost simple ailments, such as slight burns and cuts, headaches, and stomach upsets, can be satisfactorily treated at home with common sense and some generic medical supplies. An emergency kit made up of a few reliable ointments and solutions, a pain reliever, bandages, a thermometer, and some simple tools will generally prove adequate. However, when the home remedy does not work or it is apparent that the problem is too serious for home care, see your doctor.

Some shelf space, preferably in the bathroom and preferably with a door that will either lock or is well out of reach of children, should be used for medical supplies. The space should be kept orderly, and everything should be well marked. If an open shelf is used, make sure to wash and wipe nose droppers, spoons, open salve tubes, and the like before use. Following are some first-aid essentials for your medicine chest.

**Cuts and Abrasions**
- ✔ Antibacterial soap
- ✔ Adhesive bandages of various sizes
- ✔ Roll of adhesive tape
- ✔ Sterile dressings (especially 4 x 4-inch gauze pads)
- ✔ Roll of 4-inch gauze (to hold dressings)
- ✔ Pair of blunt-end scissors

**Burns (Minor)**
✔ Burn ointment or spray

**Skin Problems**
✔ Hydrocortisone cream or calamine lotion (itches and rashes)
✔ Petroleum jelly
✔ Antifungal powder or spray for athlete's foot
✔ Sunscreen and sunburn spray
✔ Insect repellent

**Poison (Swallowed)**
Use only after consulting a physician or poison-control center.
✔ Syrup of ipecac (to induce vomiting)
✔ Activated charcoal (to absorb poison that should not be regurgitated)
✔ Epsom salts (to speed excretion of poison)

**Heat Exhaustion**
✔ Sodium bicarbonate (mix a pinch with ¼ teaspoon salt and 1 quart water and drink)

**Pain Relief**
✔ Aspirin or other over-the-counter pain reliever (acetaminophen for children and pregnant women)

**Miscellaneous**
✔ Surgical tweezers for removing splinters
✔ Cotton balls
✔ Elastic bandage for sprains
✔ Ice bag to reduce swelling
✔ Hot-water bottle and heating pad for aches and pains
✔ Thermometer
✔ Sodium bicarbonate for bee, ant, and wasp stings

# Emergency Car Kit

✔ Battery-powered radio, flashlight, and extra batteries
✔ Blanket
✔ Booster cables
✔ Fire extinguisher (five-pound A-B-C type)
✔ First-aid kit and manual
✔ Bottled water and nonperishable high-energy foods such as granola bars, raisins, and peanut butter
✔ Maps, shovel, and flares
✔ Tire repair kit and pump

⋘⋙

*Why should we not try to make our children enjoy their home? Try to avoid all unnecessary fault-finding, and especially abstain from it at mealtimes. It tends to destroy the appetite, not only of the poor offender, but of all the rest of the family. Give a pleasant greeting to all in the morning, and at night, and when meeting at the table. Do not be stingy of kisses. It is better to put them at interest than to hoard them.*

— THE OLD FARMER'S ALMANAC, 1882

# HINTS & SUGGESTIONS

### Family Matters

☞ To pick up bits and pieces of broken glass safely, rub a damp bar of soap over the area where glass has splintered. Then shave off the surface of the soap to which the glass has adhered. Wrap these soap "peelings" in newspaper and discard.

☞ A drop of lemon juice rubbed on insect bites or stings instantly relieves the irritation.

☞ To lubricate a stubborn zipper, rub soap on both sides while closed. Then unzip and rub soap over the open teeth.

☞ A few elastic bands around a drinking glass offer small hands a better grip.

☞ To relieve a sunburn, add ¼ cup baking soda and ½ cup cornstarch to a warm, not hot, bath.

*There are times when only a dog will do*
*For a friend…when you're beaten sick and blue*
*And the world's all wrong, for he won't care*
*If you break and cry, or grouch and swear,*
*For he'll let you know as he licks your hands*
*That he's downright sorry…and he understands.*

— DON BLANDING (1894–?)

# Eight Rules for Pet Owners

"All you really need in life is the love of a good cat," cartoonist George Booth noted in *The New Yorker*. Millions of us would agree, perhaps amending the sentiment to include the loyalty of a good dog. We love our pets and spend millions of dollars every year to feed and nurture them. But at the same time, according to a number of experienced veterinarians we talked to, many pet lovers make mistakes that endanger the health, and sometimes even the lives, of animals. Here are a few problem areas they discussed with us.

## 1. Don't Feed Cats or Dogs Milk

Neither cats nor dogs have the proper enzyme to digest cow's milk. They don't need milk, and although it may not do them a great deal of harm, any dairy product can cause chronic diarrhea that can make them miserable. Drinking milk can be harmful to male cats because its mineral content may cause crystal formation and other problems in the urinary tract.

It's far better to feed your pet a low-ash pet food, but be sure the percentage of ash is calculated on a dry-weight basis — some manufacturers dilute pet food with water to make it look more healthful.

## 2. Petproof Your House & Yard

Think of pets as being as vulnerable as small children and keep dangerous substances out of their reach. Pets can be intoxicated by prescription drugs meant for human beings or by any toxic substances around the house or garage.

Antifreeze, for instance, is extremely poisonous to pets and yet has an attractive flavor. It quickly causes kidney failure, and the odds of reviving a dog poisoned with antifreeze are poor. Some unlucky dogs sample the sweet-tasting stuff from a puddle in a driveway or the toilet of a summer house just opened for the season. Do you feel the need to do some lobbying? One vet told us, "For about a penny a gallon, antifreeze manufacturers could give the stuff a bitter flavor and save the lives of thousands of dogs."

Pennies are toxic, too. The zinc added to the copper is poisonous to pets (and small children). Dogs often have an enthusiastic tendency to ingest indigestible foreign objects that may have to be removed surgically. One vet keeps on his desk a glass jar of widgets he and his colleagues have removed from doggy digestive systems. The jar has held "everything from fishhooks and diamond rings — more than one — to an entire butcher knife."

Cats are less likely than dogs to eat metal objects, but they are more likely to ingest stringy things. String winds around a cat's intestines and can be deadly. Cat keepers should keep string, thread, rubber bands, and Christmas tinsel out of cats' reach. Don't put icicles on your Christmas tree if you have a cat. One vet removed four yards of string from the intestine of one kitty and a threaded needle from the esophagus of another.

## 3. Don't Play Doctor

When a pet is ill and its owner tries home remedies, it's usually no kindness. Consult your vet. Animals have special needs. A classic mistake is giving acetaminophen to a cat. Cats lack the proper enzyme to digest it, and even one tablet can kill a full-grown animal. Likewise, aspirin can make cats sick. The average adult cat can tolerate one-quarter of an adult aspirin every three days.

Our vets reported that people try the weirdest things for fleas, and some of them, such as gasoline and patchouli oil, are toxic. Most of the vets recommend flea powders and baths rather than flea collars.

## 4. Bathe Dogs & Cats

Some people think dogs never need to be bathed, but they do. Some need monthly baths, some weekly, depending on the oil and dander each builds up. Use a pet shampoo that's pH balanced for pets. Pet skin has a different pH than human skin.

Bathing cats is a good idea, especially if their human companions are allergic to dander. You can purchase a spray-on product that will hold dander in place until the weekly bath.

If you think cats hate water, you may be wrong. "It's surprising how many cats seem to enjoy a bath," one vet said. "Just use warm water, start quietly at their feet, and don't splash water into their faces."

## 5. Don't Overfeed Your Pets

When it comes to feeding pets, the number one mistake is overfeeding. Some people like a fat animal, but overfeeding them is really killing them with kindness. In nature, nearly all animals regulate their own weight, but in a domestic situation, they will overeat. Cats do better than dogs at self-feeding.

Vets agree that it's tough to keep a pet on a diet. "It's very hard to cajole a cat to exercise more, but you can try a low-ash diet for cats, especially male cats."

## 6. Beware of Home-Cooked Treats

If you're frying chicken livers and braising short ribs for your pets, you're making a mistake — even if they like your cooking. Giving pets "people food" leads to an unbalanced diet, as does letting them dictate what they eat. If a dog is given nothing but meat (with the best of intentions), it will lead to a calcium phosphate imbalance that can promote bone disease. Pay special attention to small dogs, who are particularly good at manipulating their owners and holding out for special foods.

High-fat table scraps also can cause inflammation of the pancreas, a sometimes fatal illness. Vets report an increase in cases at Thanksgiving from turkey scraps, at Easter from ham, and in summer from ice cream.

## 7. Don't Give Your Dog a Bone

Real bones can get lodged in a dog's throat or digestive tract, even though such instances are rarely fatal. "Rawhide bones are great for a dog's teeth and gums," one vet said. "Chewing rawhide cleans the teeth, and in a clinical study conducted at Harvard, even giving unlimited rawhide bones produced no gastrointestinal problems."

## 8. Don't Leave Your Pets Out in the Cold

Cold weather takes an extra toll on pets, so go ahead and pamper yours a bit. "Some breeds of dog do OK outside in the bitter cold," one doctor said, "but it's not really in their best interest. It's a mistake to leave dogs and cats out at night in the cold; it puts a lot of stress on them. And cold, wet footing can lead to cracks and soreness. When your pet comes in from the cold, wash all the road salt off his feet and apply a cream." It's not necessary to use anything by Lancôme; bag balm will do.

## DOGGY DEMEANOR

| Gentlest Breeds | Fiercest Breeds | Smartest Breeds | Most Popular Breeds |
|---|---|---|---|
| Golden retriever | Pit bull | Border collie | Labrador retriever |
| Labrador retriever | German shepherd | Poodle | Rottweiler |
| Shetland sheepdog | (Alsatian) | German shepherd | Cocker spaniel |
| Old English sheep- | Husky | Golden retriever | German shepherd |
| dog | Malamute | Doberman pinscher | Poodle |
| Welsh terrier | Doberman pinscher | Shetland sheepdog | Golden retriever |
| Yorkshire terrier | Rottweiler | Labrador retriever | Beagle |
| Beagle | Great Dane | Papillon | Dachshund |
| Dalmatian | Saint Bernard | Rottweiler | Shetland sheepdog |
| Pointer | | Australian cattle | Chow |
| | | dog | |

# Why Do Cats Eat Grass?   *BY LAURA A. KLURE*

In the absence of conclusive research, veterinarians and other experts are nonetheless willing to offer opinions on the answer to this question.

Susan McDonough, in her book *The Complete Book of Questions Cat Owners Ask Their Vet, and Answers* (Running Press, 1980), states, "Cats like to eat grass, and sometimes they eat it when they have mild gastritis — for instance, when a hairball is bothering them. Usually they'll vomit soon after that, and this has led to the belief that cats eat grass when they're sick to make themselves vomit. Actually, it's probably a local irritation that causes vomiting, rather than the cat 'understanding' that it 'needs' to vomit."

According to Dr. Ken Decroo, owner of the Wild Animal Training Center in Riverside, California, some domestic cats and captive exotic cats eat grass because they're not getting enough of the plant material they would normally get from their prey. He has observed grass or bamboo eating by many captive cats, including cougars, lions, jaguars, tigers, small leopard cats, and leopards, who have been deprived of plant material normally obtained by their eating entrails (which most cats usually consume before any other part of their victims).

In *The Well Cat Book* (Random House, 1975), Terri McGinnis agrees that "grass eating is often an 'enjoyable pastime' for cats and not a sign of illness." Similar sentiments were expressed by Patricia Curtis, particularly with regard to indoor cats eating houseplants, although she does point out that "some cats will chew plants when they're angry at the owners." In *The Indoor Cat* (Doubleday, 1981), she also writes that "some properly fed cats like to nibble on plants (and grass) just for the hell of it."

## Don't Poison Your Pussycat

The following common houseplants are poisonous to cats:

- ✔ Azalea (*Rhododendron*)
- ✔ Common or cherry laurel (*Prunus laurocerasus*)
- ✔ Dumb cane (*Dieffenbachia*)
- ✔ Elephant's ear (*Caladium*)
- ✔ Mistletoe (*Viscum album*)
- ✔ Oleander (*Nerium oleander*)
- ✔ Philodendron (*Philodendron*)
- ✔ Poinsettia (*Euphorbia pulcherrima*)
- ✔ True ivy (*Hedera*)
- ✔ Winter or false Jerusalem cherry (*Solanum capsicastrum*)

# CARPET CAT-ASTROPHE!
### or What to Do When Your Pet Makes a Wet Boo-boo on the Carpet

**1.** Blot the affected area with clean white cloths or paper towels until none of the urine shows on the absorbent material.

**2.** Use a spray bottle or a sponge to lightly flush the area with tap water. Do not overwet the carpet.

**3.** Blot dry with the same type of absorbent material.

**4.** Combine 1 teaspoon dishwashing powder detergent and 1 cup lukewarm water. Rub the solution into the carpet pile with your fingers.

**5.** Blot dry, then flush as described in step 2. Blot until the area is as dry as possible.

**6.** Dampen the area with a solution of equal parts water and white vinegar. Let sit for a few minutes. Blot until the carpet is as dry as possible.

**7.** Place a one-inch layer of the absorbent material on the treated area and weight it down with a heavy object. Leave it in place for eight hours.
— *A. S. Garstein*

# HINTS & SUGGESTIONS

### Pets

☛ If your cat scratches at your furniture, rub the wooden areas with fresh lemon balm leaves. The cat will stay away, and the wood will look as though you've just polished it.

☛ Add a few drops of apple cider vinegar to your dog's drinking water to encourage a glossy pelt and temper doggy odor.

☛ If your goldfish are logy and grumpy, put them in a quart of fresh water with a teaspoon of salt and let them swim around for 15 minutes. They'll be new fish!

☛ To deter dogs from tearing open trash bags, add a few drops of chlorine bleach to the bag before closing. Dogs don't like the smell.

# Chapter 6

# Cockroaches to Telemarketers,
## or Useful Tactics Against Pests Ancient & Modern

*The flea, though he kill none, he does all the harm he can.*
*— JOHN DONNE (1572–1631)*

*Y*OU MAY THINK YOUR HOME IS YOURS ALONE, BUT there are those who would dispute that claim. At some point, you've probably had to contend with wasps or hornets in your attic, ants in your pantry, cockroaches in your kitchen, or some other insect species seemingly bent on taking the place over. Perhaps you've been invaded by mice. If you live in a fairly rural area, you may have been plagued by garden-despoiling raccoons or garbage-picking skunks.

No matter where you live, you have certainly been pestered by another sort of household intruder — the telephone salesperson. This is especially vexing because the problem is so recent that there's no accepted body of information on how best to deal with it. Most people know how to get rid of carpenter ants (poison them with boric acid) or discourage raccoons from raiding the vegetable garden (leave a radio tuned to an all-night talk show between the rows of corn), but few have any inkling of how to humanely dispatch unwanted telephone callers. Fortunately, it's not a difficult skill to acquire. With a little practice, you'll soon find yourself handling even the wiliest light bulb salesman with ease. But before we look at some proven techniques, let's consider some tactics that *don't* work.

Forget about technological solutions, such as the increasingly popular tactic of using an answering machine to screen incoming calls. Under this plan, the caller is greeted by a message that says something like "You have reached Jane Smith's telephone. Either I'm not here right now or I *am* here and I just don't want to talk to you. But if you think I might want to call you back, please leave a message at the beep." There are at least two problems with this approach. The first is that it fosters a sort of bunker mentality — the feeling that the outside world is an unpleasant, threatening place that requires you to barricade yourself inside your own home. The second is that although an answering machine will discourage telemarketers, it also will discourage everyone else. A year or so after setting it up, you'll begin to wonder why your friends never call. That message could be the reason.

Then there are machines that display the caller's number before you answer, and other machines that deliver a canned message requesting that your name and number be removed from the caller's files before automatically hanging up. Beware. Although such devices may seem to work well in the short run, they actually make the whole problem worse by fostering a sort of telecommunications arms race.

That's because the people who develop such equipment aren't humanitarians. Like manufacturers who sell airplanes to one warring country and antiaircraft guns to its adversary, they're in business to supply whatever the market demands. As a result, callers who suspect that you might not want to hear from them can invest in a machine of their own designed to block your machine's attempt to display their numbers — leaving you to invest even more in a machine that will reject incoming calls whose numbers have been blocked. It's hard to say where all this will end, but these folks certainly don't need any more encouragement than they're already getting.

Another approach that doesn't work is banging down the receiver or otherwise abusing unwanted callers. Admittedly, this will free up the phone quickly, but beyond that it has nothing to recommend it. If you've ever succumbed to that impulse in a moment of irritation, you've probably found that your conscience bothered you about it for some time. And although you may have tried to convince yourself otherwise, this is not an example of a conscience with too much free time on its hands.

The truth is that your conscience knows something that you may have overlooked: no matter how annoying it is to be called away from the dinner table by an amazing offer on case lots of glow-in-the-dark gladiolus bulbs, you're still dealing with a fellow human being — who probably isn't enjoying the call any more than you are. Telemarketing is a tedious, thankless job, and venting your frustrations on such callers is just plain wrong.

That's not to say that you need to listen to the entire sales pitch. Unless you're actually thinking of buying something — which is highly unlikely — the kindest thing you can do is to politely tell the caller that you're not interested and quietly hang up.

Although that sort of dry, formulaic approach will work, it's more fun for everyone if you show some imagination. If you can manage it, try to come up with an interesting explanation for why you can't possibly avail yourself of the product or service being offered.

Isn't that dishonest? Not at all. Such exchanges are not meant to be taken literally by either party. The caller is working from a fanciful script, which assumes that (1) you regularly buy things from telephone salespeople, (2) you're happy to drop what you are doing to give careful consideration to whatever the caller has to offer, and (3) the caller is genuinely enthusiastic about offering you such a wonderful opportunity.

In the world of telemarketing, facts need not be strictly factual — which is why the caller for a rival long-distance phone company can excitedly promise you cheaper rates just seconds into your conversation. You might ask how he can be sure of that, when he has no idea what you're paying now, but that would be abrupt and rude.

Remember, your goal is not to put the caller on the spot but to wrap things up as quickly as possible while allowing both parties to save face. And the fairest way to do that is by countering the caller's script with an equally imaginative one of your own. Here are a few possibilities that have been found to work:

*Remember, your goal is not to put the caller on the spot but to wrap things up as quickly as possible while allowing both parties to save face.*

> "I won't be able to take advantage of that because I'm beginning a ten-year sentence for mail fraud later this week. I don't want to make any commitments until after I'm released."

> "I'm sorry, but this house is about to be torn down for a highway project, and we'll be moving back to Labrador."

> "Thanks for calling, but the Social Security Administration just declared me legally dead. My bank accounts are frozen, and my lawyer thinks it might take a year or so to get the whole thing straightened out."

"I'm sorry, but this whole side of town is about to be abandoned because of a toxic waste problem. I'm not sure where I'll be going after that."

You may want to copy these lines — and any useful variants you develop yourself — on a cue card that can be left taped to the wall for easy reference. Scripted lines need not be especially plausible, but they should not be obviously specious. Avoid explanations such as "Sorry, I don't have a telephone" or "I'm sorry, but I don't speak English."

*You'll know you've perfected your delivery when you begin to notice a brief, respectful pause after you deliver your lines, as the caller pays silent tribute to your mastery of the situation.*

Try for a sincere, heartfelt delivery. Telemarketers work hard at giving every caller their best shot, and they deserve no less from you. That's especially important at the close, when you ask the caller to delete your name from the company's files. (Don't forget this step; telemarketers are legally obligated to do so if asked.) You should try to convey the impression that although you regret being crossed off the list, you can't in good conscience expect to remain on it, given the circumstances you've just described.

If you do all that correctly, you should be able to limit most calls to thirty seconds or less. You'll know you've perfected your delivery when you begin to notice a brief, respectful pause after you deliver your lines, as the caller pays silent tribute to your mastery of the situation. You can be forgiven for feeling deeply satisfied at such times.

From time to time, you may even encounter a caller who reveals a flash of irritation as she realizes how thoroughly she has been outflanked. You may detect a hint of sarcasm in her voice as she says good-bye. She may angrily hang up on you without a word. Don't take it personally. The poor woman is probably just having a bad day. And with any luck, her conscience will bother her about it later.

*Men should stop fighting amoung themselves and
start fighting insects*

— *LUTHER BURBANK (1849–1926)*

# Carpenter Ants & Termites     BY EARL PROULX

Carpenter ants and subterranean termites are both notorious wood
destroyers, but there are important differences between them. Carpenter
ants, unlike termites, do not eat or digest the cellulose in the wood they
remove. Their sole purpose in removing the wood is to create space for
their colonies. Termites are very messy eaters. They leave their tunnels
clogged with organic grit, dead termite bodies, and fecal matter.
By comparison, carpenter ants are fussy housekeepers. They
leave their tunnels looking as if they've been sandpapered. (You
know they are there because of the little piles of sawdust they
leave beneath their holes.)

The insects themselves are easy to tell apart. Most termites — if you ever see them — are tiny, white, and thick-
waisted. They look like grains of rice with legs, mandibles, and
straight antennae composed of strings of tiny beads. Since exposure to
open air rapidly evaporates their body liquids and causes death, you will
rarely, if ever, see them working aboveground. In contrast, carpenter ants
do work aboveground. A carpenter ant is much larger than a termite and
black in color. It has a wasplike waist and bent "elbowed" antennae. The queens of both species are black and have wings, but even
here the differences in the waists and antennae are still apparent.

You can identify a termite problem in another way, too. Look
for mud tunnels on the foundation walls — in the cellar, outside,
or under your porch. Subterranean termites, which live underground in
colonies, come up through these tunnels during the day to feed. The tunnels are about one-half inch wide, semicircular, and built from the ground
up to woodwork. They can be inside the house — on posts in the cellar, for
instance — as well as outside. If you find any tunnels, check with a local
exterminator about treating the foundation area.

# The Cockroach,
# or A Lesson in Survival
*BY RICHARD ROMEO*

Cockroaches have lived with humans for so long that it is difficult to say where the various species originated. We do know that cockroaches have been around for 350 million years, which is about 348 million years longer than we have.

According to entomologists, the closest living relative of the cockroach is the praying mantis, which is a highly specialized predator of other insects. Praying mantises are more distantly related to termites, which seem to have branched off on their own about 100 million years ago.

Unlike termites and mantises, however, cockroaches have not succeeded by specializing but by evolving into extremely efficient generalists, capable of filling almost any environmental niche that happens to open up. This is most evident in the matter of diet. Individual cockroach species do seem to have their favorite foods — German cockroaches prefer sugars and carbohydrates, Oriental cockroaches enjoy bookbindings, and brown-banded cockroaches love a hearty meal of glue from the backs of stamps and envelope flaps — but this does not stop any of them from eating almost anything else organic that will stand still long enough.

Besides eating all types of human foods, whether liquid or solid, cockroaches readily eat pet food, toothpaste, love letters, wool, and the empty egg cases and droppings of other cockroaches, not to mention dead or disabled members of their own species. They dislike cucumbers.

In short, cockroaches are extremely good at what they do. This includes driving humans crazy. As a result, we tend to be less interested in controlling cockroaches than in killing, smashing, and destroying them. Unfortunately, that's much easier to fantasize about than it is to accomplish.

For one thing, cockroaches are nocturnal and work mostly under cover of darkness. They scatter instantly when the lights go on, and although they have little endurance, they are tough to beat in a

sprint. (When going flat out, cockroaches have been clocked at about one foot per second.) And a short burst of speed is usually all that's needed, since cockroaches seldom venture far from their hiding places and have an almost uncanny ability to take refuge in tight spots. Even the king-size American cockroach, measuring up to two inches long, can squeeze through a crack no wider than the thickness of a dime. And although you may not have realized it, most household cockroaches can fly reasonably well, though they seldom bother.

In addition to being sensitive to light, cockroaches are quick to detect the slight air movements that telegraph approaching trouble, thanks to specialized sensing hairs on their abdomens. The vibration of an approaching footstep also will send cockroaches running for cover; they can detect movements of less than one-millionth millimeter in the surface on which they stand. And to make matters worse, individuals of some species alert their companions of approaching danger by rattling their forewings and dragging the spurs at the ends of their tibiae over the ground before emitting foul-smelling glandular secretions to cover their retreat.

Hundreds of millions of years of close contact with tropical vegetation and exposure to potent plant toxins have left cockroaches with an unnerving ability to become resistant to chemical poisons. Many widely used, once-effective pesticides, such as chlordane, are now all but useless against household roaches. Spraying an insecticide often does produce a short-lived decrease in the cockroach population, but that's because the little devils take up temporary quarters in another room — or at your neighbor's place — only to come scuttling back once the coast is clear.

Purveyors of pesticides and the newer roach baits love to suggest that final victory over the cockroach is just around the corner. This is just hot air. In truth, the best we can hope for is localized tactical superiority — and even then, poison alone won't do the job. Following are the far more important moves in any campaign against household cockroaches.

## What to Do

- ☛ Disrupt their supply lines. Make sure that pet food, garbage, and dirty dishes are not left exposed, especially overnight. Don't overlook obvious food sources. The crumb-catching tray inside your toaster and the spill trays beneath the burners of your kitchen range may provide enough food for an army of cockroaches.

- ☛ Store bulk food in glass, plastic, or metal containers. Throw away stamps and envelopes. (If you're at war with cockroaches, you won't have time for reading or writing letters anyway.)

- ☛ Make a concerted effort to close off potential entry points and daytime hiding places. Use caulking compound to seal cracks around baseboards and cabinets, being particularly attentive to gaps where plumbing pipes penetrate walls or floors. Deny the cockroaches access to water by repairing any leaky pipes or fixtures and insulating exposed cold-water pipes that drip condensation in hot weather. And because cockroaches often hide out in the traps beneath sink drains — especially kitchen sinks, where food particles tend to collect — leave a tight-fitting strainer basket in the drain opening at all times.

- ☛ If further action is needed, this is the time to mop up any survivors with poisoned baits, which administer a lethal dose of poison to cockroaches that actually feed on them. The most effective poison currently used in roach baits is a compound called hydramethylnon. Although it is not harmful to warm-blooded animals, it is highly toxic to cockroaches, killing not only those that feed directly on the bait but also those that feed on the bodies of the poisoned roaches.

- ☛ Once your home is relatively roach free, avoid transporting new roaches inside in food containers, trash, or used appliances. This is not merely a theoretical possibility. The brown-banded cockroach was almost exclusively a southern pest until after World War II, when it spread to the rest of the country by hiding in the household goods of military personnel transferred to the North.

༄༅༅

*Cockroaches and socialites are the only things that can stay up all night and eat anything.*

—HERB CAEN (1916–1997)

༄༅༅

# THE CRICKET ON YOUR HEARTH

The best that can be said for the house cricket is that it does not do all that much harm. It will eat any sort of food and many organic materials, including magazines, books, and cotton clothing, but it does not bite or sting and is only a minor transmitter of disease. And its nocturnal chirping drives only *some* people crazy. That's about as faint as praise gets, but it seems to be enough for cricket lovers.

*Acheta domestica* is originally native to North Africa and adjacent regions of the Mediterranean. Unlike many species of hardy North American crickets, house crickets cannot survive cold winter weather without human help. They prefer temperatures between 80° and 85° F, which is why they often live in places such as bakeries, furnace rooms, commercial laundries, and hearths. To show its gratitude for being provided with a warm place to live, a cricket will sing to you all winter long, whether you want it to or not.

The cricket produces its song by elevating its front wings and rubbing the hardened portion, or scraper, of one wing against the ridged, filelike portion of the other wing. It is difficult for a human to locate a singing cricket by sound. That's just as well for the cricket. You can, however, determine the temperature (°F) in its hiding place: count the number of chirps for 14 seconds and add 40.

— *Richard Romeo*

# Homespun Remedies for Fleas

You know you're in trouble when (1) certain areas of your carpet seem to hop, (2) sitting on the couch becomes an experience in acupuncture, and (3) your dog and cat act like animal contortionists in their efforts to scratch and bite six itches at once. In other words, your house has become a giant fleabag.

Unfortunately, commercial insecticides are often not only smelly and poisonous to other life forms but also ineffective. Fleas, highly specialized bloodsucking parasites with the evolutionary hardiness of cockroaches, have become resistant to the pesticides commonly found in insect bombs and flea collars. In fact, many veterinarians advise pet owners not to waste their money on these items. But there's more than one way to flummox a flea, and we are pleased to offer a few suggestions.

☛ Vacuum rugs and upholstered furniture daily to remove fleas, eggs, and larvae. Fleas spend most of their time away from their hosts and can survive for several weeks without feeding, so keep up the vacuuming diligently for at least a month. Be sure to block up any exits from the vacuum cleaner lest the fleas hop back out. Vacuum your pets if they will let you. (Some love it; some would sooner die a horrible death.)

☛ Add minced fresh garlic or garlic powder and a sprinkling of brewer's yeast to your pet's food to repel fleas.

☛ Construct a flea trap that makes use of two basic facts about fleas: they are attracted to light, and they can't swim. To make the trap, fill a dinner plate or shallow soup bowl with water and a squirt of dishwashing detergent and place it on the floor in an area frequented by your dog or cat. Position a gooseneck lamp over the bowl with the light about six inches over the surface of the water. At night, when the rest of the house is dark, turn on the light and leave it on all night. Fleas will leap toward the light and fall into the water. The detergent will have lowered the surface tension of the water so that the fleas will sink and drown.

☛ Your veterinarian can supply you with a nonaerosol flea spray for pets based on the chemical pyrethrum, which is extracted from the dried heads of certain varieties of chrysanthemums. Your vet also may have a rug and upholstery nonaerosol spray that microencapsulates tiny drops of an effective insecticide.

☛ Many pets are made miserable not only by the flea bites themselves but also by an allergic reaction to flea saliva, a persistent condition that is often treated with cortisone-related medication.

☛ For the most effective control of fleas, start early in the spring and be diligent. With any luck, your fleas will flee.

## A Few Facts About the

# Infamous Flea

☛ Fleas can jump vertically or horizontally 150 times their own length. This is equivalent to a human jumping 1,000 feet.

☛ Flea bodies can withstand tremendous pressure, their secret to surviving the scratching and biting of the flea-ridden host.

☛ Fleas are covered with bristles and spines that point backward. That's why it's so difficult to pick a flea from your pet's fur.

☛ As carriers of plague (transmitted by fleas from infected rats to humans), fleas have killed more people than all the wars ever fought.

# A Fly in Your Buttermilk?

*F*lies are often found in houses. But not all house flies are houseflies *(Musca domestica)*. In the autumn, rural and suburban homes are often invaded by the cluster fly *(Pollenia rudis)*, which resembles the housefly so closely that few people can tell the difference between them.

Their shape provides the most reliable clue. The cluster fly folds its wings together when at rest, giving it an oval-shaped silhouette when seen from above. The housefly, by contrast, holds its wings slightly apart, giving it a rakish, V-shaped silhouette reminiscent of a delta wing fighter jet.

That difference is mirrored in their behavior. Cluster flies are inept and sluggish. They have no interest in food but are irresistibly attracted to light, and they may drive you to distraction by buzzing incessantly around a light bulb or against a window. Although they are easily massacred by a strip of flypaper near a light source, they don't deserve it. They are bewildered little beasts who don't really want to be in your house at all.

Cluster flies ordinarily live on nectar. When the weather grows cold, they work their way into crevices in tree bark, where they gather in tightly packed clusters to wait for spring. A cluster fly that crawls into a crack in the clapboarded outside wall of your house, however, may continue crawling until it emerges in the perpetual springtime of your living room. Not knowing what else to do, it will beat its wings fruitlessly against the window, trying to get outside and go about its business.

It will keep buzzing against the glass until it drops dead of exhaustion or until squashed by an annoyed homeowner — or perhaps until some compassionate soul opens the window and lets it out. At that point, it will feel the chill in the outside air, find a new crack in the siding, and begin working its way back in. The cluster fly is something of a tragic figure.

The housefly, by contrast, is a hard-bitten opportunist. Admittedly, it is fastidious in its personal habits. According to entomologist H. J. Heinz, houseflies habitually engage in seven types of cleaning behavior: head cleaning, proboscis cleaning, foreleg cleaning, hind leg cleaning, wing cleaning, abdomen cleaning, and middle leg cleaning. That pretty well covers it.

You'd want to spend a lot of

time cleaning yourself, too, if you were a fly. Houseflies feed on garbage and liquefied, decomposed matter of all kinds. Their mouth parts — which have evolved into a sort of sponging, sopping apparatus — require them to subsist on a liquid diet. But like so many dieters, the housefly is a resourceful little devil. When it encounters a piece of hard candy or a slice of pound cake, it disgorges the liquid remnants of its last meal, then slurps the newly dissolved material back up. It may play with its food for some time, like a kindergartner with a straw and a carton of milk.

Each of the housefly's six legs has two lobes and two claws on the tarsus. These are known as the pulvilli, and they enable the fly to walk on walls and ceilings, although scientists still do not know exactly how. High-speed photography, however, has laid bare another aspect of housefly locomotion.

It was long assumed that a fly landed on a ceiling by performing a barrel roll in the final split second of approach, enabling it to touch down with feet uppermost. We now know better. The fly actually approaches the ceiling right side up, at a shallow angle. Just as its back is about to strike the surface overhead, it reaches up with its front legs, makes contact with the ceiling, does a neat half somersault, and — ta da! — comes to rest upside down, facing the direction from which it came.

As its Latin name, *Musca domestica,* suggests, the housefly is basically a homebody. In the course of a two-month lifetime, few flies venture more than a few hundred yards from their hatch sites. If you can eliminate fly-breeding sites near your home — rotting carcasses, piles of cannery waste, open sewers, and the like — you can keep the number of flies around you to a minimum.

— *Richard Romeo*

## The Prolific Housefly

Under ideal conditions, authorities say, 336 trillion houseflies (it would take 31,688 years for a person to count to 1 trillion) could develop from a single pair in one April-to-September season, if they all survived. How fortunate it is that their increase is limited by temperature, humidity, wind, and living organisms that kill countless numbers.

*— Herb Saltford*

# Fly Liquidator

*By this method, kitchens may be kept clear of flies all summer without the danger attending poison.*

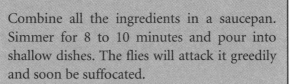

1 pint milk
¼ pound raw sugar
2 ounces ground pepper

Combine all the ingredients in a saucepan. Simmer for 8 to 10 minutes and pour into shallow dishes. The flies will attack it greedily and soon be suffocated.

Adapted from an unidentified news clip (probably from a central Massachusetts newspaper) kept in an unpublished recipe book, c. 1850.

## THE BATTLE OF THE MOTHS

Clothes moths fly about and deposit their eggs during almost any season in our heated homes, but in April special attention should be given to this most important matter. When the approach of warmer days invites us to shed overcoats, sweaters, and extra blankets, we do not always take care of these things promptly, and moths get at them while they are waiting for attention. The moths lay their eggs, and the larvae or worms that hatch out do the damage by feeding on woolens and furs.

Why not clear out at least one closet, suggest entomologists of the U.S. Department of Agriculture, and devote it entirely to the storage of winter garments and furnishings? If everything can be put away at once, the task is simplified. Clean, brush thoroughly, and sun each article to make sure there are no hidden moth eggs in it. Place the garments on hangers and sprinkle the floor with a moth repellent. Then lock the door and seal the cracks with tape. If the garments must be put away one at a time, it is better to wrap each article in strong, unbroken wrapping paper (after cleaning and sunning) with the ends turned under. —*The Old Farmer's Almanac*, 1935

# Homemade Moth Repellent

*This repellent is a nice change from mothballs.*

    1 handful each dried thyme, tansy, peppermint, pennyroyal,
      and whole cloves
    2 handfuls each dried lavender, southernwood, santolina,
      and lemon rind
    1 tablespoon powdered orrisroot
    several drops lemon or clove oil

Combine all the ingredients and spoon into cheesecloth or cotton bags, filling each bag with about ½ cup repellent. Hang the bags in closets or over hangers that hold your woolens.

# The House Mouse

*BY RICHARD ROMEO*

House mice know their way around. They are adept at living on the fringes of human peripheral vision. This has given rise to a useful rule of thumb: if you think you saw a mouse, you did.

The modern house mouse *(Mus musculus)* apparently evolved from the Bactrian mouse of central Asia, where it lived a hardy outdoor life and subsisted on a wholesome all-natural diet of seeds and insects. Then humans arrived on the scene. They began practicing agriculture, and soon they were pretty good at it. These developments were not lost on the ancestors of today's house mice.

Unlike most small mammals, the house mouse is capable of living and propagating in a man-made environment that is altogether different from the one in which it evolved. If necessary, however, house mice can go back to roughing it. When forced to live outdoors, they are relatively nonterritorial, moving from food source to food source and constantly testing and exploring new habitats.

Put them in a warm kitchen, though, and everything changes. Before you know it, the males begin scent-marking their boundaries and aggressively driving off other males. As many as 10 females, however, will be invited to remain. Three weeks later, they will give birth to 3 to 12 young apiece.

House mice can be trapped or poisoned, but neither of these approaches strikes at the root of the problem. The best way to get rid of mice is to cut their supply lines. Don't leave food where they can get at it, and pay special attention to items that *you* may not think of as food but mice certainly will. This includes bags of pet food, grass or vegetable seeds, and birdseed. If necessary, transfer foods originally packaged in chewable cardboard to metal canisters or glass jars.

That degree of mouseproofing will not be needed for long. House mice are pragmatists. If there's nothing to eat at your house, they'll move on and try their luck next door. That's too bad for your neighbors, but that's life.

# RAT CONTROL

It is no disgrace to have rats. It is a disgrace to keep them. The female rat has from 18 to 98 offspring each year. The best time for a poison campaign is in the fall. To catch a rat, appeal to its thirst, hunger, sex drive, or curiosity. Remember, it can reach up to 18 inches, and it can jump up 3 feet and out more than 15. Rats can burrow down 5 feet or climb a vertical wall or rusty 3-inch pipe.

To do away with them, keep all garbage in metal containers with tight-fitting lids. Destroy nests and hiding places. Ratproof your buildings with screen doors. Also screen all windows, vents, transoms, exhaust openings in foundations or roofs, chimneys, and ventilators.

Red squill baits or traps are best for ridding the house of a rat. Use traps if you have pets or children around or if you don't want unseemly odors.

— *The Old Farmer's Almanac,* 1951

# An Antisquirrel Hint

If you have trouble with squirrels eating all the birdseed in your feeders, string a heavy wire between the two outside walls of your house or between two trees. On the wire, string *used* wooden or plastic spools of thread, with the bird feeder placed in the center of the wire. If a squirrel tries to climb across the wire, it will step on the spools, which will turn, and the squirrel will fall to the ground.

— *Virginia Heinrich*

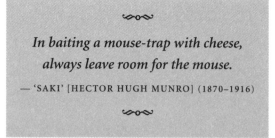

*In baiting a mouse-trap with cheese,*
*always leave room for the mouse.*

— 'SAKI' [HECTOR HUGH MUNRO] (1870–1916)

# HINTS & SUGGESTIONS

## Pest Control

☛ **Ants.** Salt or red pepper sprinkled across doorsills discourages ants from entering the house.

☛ **Flies.** A vinegar-water solution wiped on countertops repels flies. Mint on your windowsill also will keep flies away.

☛ **Insects.** Herbs can be used to deter insects in the home. Wormwood, yarrow, santolina, tansy, mint, and lavender are traditional moth repellents. Dry them and use them to fill little fabric bags, which can be tucked amid your clothing.

☛ **Moths.** "Pepper, red-cedar chips, tobacco — indeed, almost any strong, spicy smell — is good to keep moths out of your chests and drawers" (Lydia Maria Child, *The American Frugal Housewife,* 1833).

☛ **Fleas.** Try putting a drop of lemon oil on your pet's collar for flea control. Oil of rosemary also can be effective.

☛ **Fleas and Ticks.** A teaspoon of vinegar for each quart of drinking water helps keep your pet free of fleas and ticks. (This ratio of vinegar to water is for a 40-pound animal.)

☛ **Cockroaches.** "Pokeroot, boiled in water and mixed with a good quantity of molasses, set about the kitchen, the pantry & in large deep plates, will kill cockroaches in great number" (Lydia Maria Child, *The American Frugal Housewife,* 1833).

☛ **Mice.** If you see one mouse in your house, you probably have a dozen.

# Chapter 7

# Frugal *and* Happy,

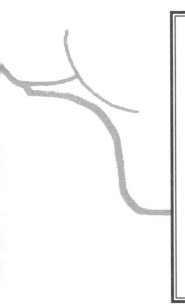

## or Strategies for the Simple Life

*Economy is going without something you do want in case you should, some day, want something you probably won't want.*

— *ANTHONY HOPE HAWKINS (1863–1933)*

*W*OULD IT MAKE YOU HAPPY TO WIN SEVERAL MILLION dollars in the state lottery? Of course it would, but it might not *keep* you happy for as long as you think. Studies show that most lottery winners, when interviewed a year later, report that they are no happier than they were before buying the winning ticket. That may strike you as astonishing, but it really shouldn't. Most people know, in their hearts, that money and happiness are only indirectly related, as a simple thought experiment will demonstrate.

Imagine two houses. The first is a glittering mansion surrounded by formal gardens, with a Rolls-Royce limousine pulled up at the grand front entrance. The second is a modest ranch house with a small vegetable garden in the backyard and an eight-year-old economy car in the driveway. Which of the two contains the happier family? It's impossible to answer that question, which isn't to say that money is not important. It is, which is why there are so many proverbs and sayings about it, including the astute observation that money doesn't matter as long as you have enough of it. And although money admittedly causes problems at times, it's a wild exaggeration to call it the root of all evil. (Besides, what the Apostle Paul actually said is that *the love of money* is the root of all evil.) It's the root of a lot of good things, too.

"Money," Ralph Waldo Emerson observed, "which represents the prose of life, and which is hardly spoken of in parlors without an apology, is in its effects and laws, as beautiful as roses." Money provides us with food, clothing, and shelter. It can be a focus of greed, but it's also the medium for works of charity. In short, it's a morally neutral tool that we can use or misuse, according to our nature.

The reason all those lottery winners aren't as happy as they thought they would be has nothing to do with the money itself but with an uncontrolled desire for the things money can buy. Even the richest person will

find that there are things he or she can't afford. Assuming that your basic physical needs have already been met, the most direct route to contentment lies not in having more but in wanting less.

That's not necessarily the same thing as living frugally, however. Frugality is basically a matter of seeking the maximum material gain for each dollar spent. Clipping coupons and searching incessantly for bargains can easily become a specialized type of greed.

So how *do* you master the nagging desire for more possessions? The short answer is that you don't. It's part of the human condition, and you're just going to have to put up with it. But it takes surprisingly little effort to bring about a noticeable improvement. Here are three practical steps you can take to control your materialistic side before it takes control of you.

**1. Wait.** In consumer goods, as in love, a period of initial restraint makes the eventual consummation that much sweeter. When you're seized by the urge to buy something, put it off for a while. Don't set a clear time limit, or you may end up standing around impatiently shifting your weight from one foot to the other while you wait for the clock to run out. (In general, the duration of the waiting period should be roughly proportional to the size of the purchase. A new car calls for longer consideration than a pair of socks or set of measuring spoons.) Don't seek expert advice, study consumer magazines, or shop around for a lower price. Just wait.

Eventually, one of two things will happen. You may decide that you really do want or need the item in question, in which case you can cheerfully go ahead and buy it with a clear conscience. With any luck, the manufacturer will have come out with an improved version while you were waiting. But you'll be surprised at how often you suddenly realize that you're getting along very well without that thing. It wasn't love; it was only infatuation. You've avoided a dead-end relationship and saved money in the bargain.

**2. Accept no substitutes.** Before you reach for your wallet, ask yourself what you really want. Do you *really* want a new pair of running shoes? Maybe you just want to be a better runner or have more free time to go running. Maybe you think that investing money in new shoes will pressure you into running more often than you otherwise might.

This is not to suggest that you're deliberately concealing your real motive or that you need some sort of therapy to put you in touch with your innermost self. The truth is that we all succumb to this sort of confusion from time to time. Maybe it's the fault of advertisers, who constantly bombard us with the message that happiness is just a matter of buying the right products. Then again, maybe it's not.

In any case, the precise cause — if there is one — isn't important. What *is* important is realizing that you can't produce happiness by spending money on something you don't really want for reasons you don't understand. Maybe you should buy a stopwatch and a book on training techniques or start getting up earlier so that you can run for an hour every morning. Maybe you should give up on running — which, let's face it, you just don't enjoy — and take up swimming. Making the right choice won't necessarily save you money, but it will keep you from suffering a twinge of regret every time you open the closet door and look at that almost-unused pair of shoes.

*You can't produce happiness by spending money on something you don't really want for reasons you don't understand.*

**3. Care about your things.** Most of us have at least one possession — that old cast-iron frying pan, frayed wool shirt, or nicely worn garden spade — that we value for reasons having nothing to do with its cost. It may have some special sentimental value, or it may simply be an everyday item that we've grown to regard as an old friend for its long and faithful service. Either way, we treat it with great respect and keep it in service for as long as we possibly can. When it's finally worn beyond repair, we mourn its passing and take to frequenting yard sales, looking for a new one just like the old one.

Isn't this a glaring example of overattachment to material things? Not really. Materialism is less a matter of being attached to your possessions than it is of being so *un*attached to them that your only source of satisfaction lies in accumulating new ones. This is known as the "paradox of possessions."

Marketers, of course, are well aware of the special appeal of cherished older items, which is why they promote a paradox of their own — that it's possible to buy instant old favorites right out of the box. This accounts for the abundance of products described by their makers as aged, faded, antiqued, burnished, and who knows what else.

Don't let that deprive you of the satisfaction of gradually producing your own old favorites the old-fashioned way. Whenever possible, buy new products that will last for a long time and age gracefully. (Admittedly, that won't always work; there's no point in getting attached to a computer that will be obsolete in two or three years.) And try to think of the things you already own as long-term companions rather than mere possessions. Take care of them. Clean them up. Fix them. You'll find that you'll feel better about your things — and yourself.

*Economy is a poor man's revenue:*
*extravagance a rich man's ruin.*

LYDIA MARIA CHILD (1802–1880)

*It is better to wear out than to rust out.*

— *BISHOP RICHARD CUMBERLAND (1632–1718)*

## FIRST AID FOR FURNITURE

☞ Hide minor scratches with a child's crayon. Or try shoe polish, nutmeats, linseed oil, iodine, or a felt-tip pen. Draw along the scratch, rub it with your finger, and polish with a soft cloth.

☞ In many cases, a wet pad and a hot iron will raise a dent in wood. Before starting, remove surface wax so that the moisture will penetrate the wood and make it swell when you place the wet pad on the surface and iron it.

☞ Treat white spots from water condensation, alcohol, or coffee with a fine abrasive such as fine steel wool or table salt and a lubricant. Rub the grain gently with the abrasive, then with mayonnaise, lard, cooking or salad oil, or petroleum jelly. When the white spots disappear, wax or polish the wood.

☞ To remove burns, scrape away the charred material with a sharp, curved-blade knife. After reaching solid wood, smooth the surface with fine sandpaper or steel wool. Clean the debris, restain the wood if necessary, and fill the gouge. Use common paste wax or, for deeper gouges, build up the surface with plastic wood or stick shellac before polishing or waxing as usual.

☞ For candle drips, wait until the wax hardens, then flick it off with a fingernail. Do not use a knife. To speed up hardening, wrap an ice cube in a clean cloth and hold it on the wax.

# Where Would We Be without Duct Tape?

*N*eed something to keep the wooden handle of an old hoe from splintering your palms? A quick fix for a leaky garden hose or water pipe, a rubber boot, or a plastic swimming pool? A patch to help an aging automobile muffler pass inspection? Something to remove dog hair from upholstery or to fix the lining hanging below the hem of your winter jacket? Reach for a roll of duct tape!

Arguably the most versatile product ever invented, duct tape serves nearly any purpose of daily life that requires a patch, seam, seal, joint, hinge, grip, wrap, or stiffening agent. Cheap, easy to cut and apply, and available everywhere, it also has such functional virtues as strength, flexibility, and water resistance. Duct tape sticks well to wood, plastic, leather, fabric, metal, fiberglass, and even asphalt.

☞ Count on this homely gray denizen of the utility drawer for hemming curtains; patching tents, tarps, screen doors, and automobile seats; hinging a wooden toy chest; keeping the feathers inside a torn down

jacket; and reinforcing the worn palms of work gloves.

☞ Make a rug from carpet samples and fasten them together on the back with duct tape.

☞ Use it to bind a splint on a dog's injured leg, repair tomato stems broken off by the same dog's rampage through the vegetable garden, or double as athletic tape.

☞ Race directors use duct tape to mark start and finish lines for footraces. Children use it to mark hopscotch squares in the schoolyard.

☞ Duct tape holds boxes, cabinet doors, and car hoods or trunks shut. It secures mirrors and photographs in their frames, seals packages for mailing, and mends wooden or rattan furniture and raffia basket handles.

☞ Wise and busy seamstresses know that it holds seams, pleats, tucks, linings, and zippers in place temporarily before stitching and stiffens collars, plackets, and cuffs.

☞ Duct tape works as a temporary patch for a broken window or windshield.

☞ It also makes a fine wrap for

bicycle handlebars, car steering wheels, or tool handles, as well as nifty jump-rope handles that prevent the rope ends from fraying.

☛ A loop of duct tape tidies a tangle of electrical cords, binds a decorative sheaf of cornstalks, and stiffens shoelace ends and the stems of dried flowers for easier arranging.

☛ A strip holds the batteries inside a Walkman when the plastic panel is lost or broken

We recently heard of a romance that was conducted primarily in an aging kayak. "I'll bring the kayak, honey; you bring the duct tape," the man would say. The kayak held together, but the couple broke up. There are some patch jobs even a roll of duct tape can't handle.

# Window Wisdom

## Patch 'Em Up!

Mosquitoes and other unwelcome pests have an uncanny way of finding their way into the house through any little tear in a screen. You can effectively bugproof your house by mending those holes.

Cut a square patch from an old screen about one-half inch larger all around than the hole you're covering. Unravel three rows of wires on all four sides and bend them at right angles (so that they look like "legs") all pointing in the same direction. Insert the patch through the screen and thread the legs back and forth on all sides. Snip off extra pieces that stick out.

For fabric screens, sew a patch onto the screen using a large-eyed needle and nylon fishing line or strong cord and securing it with a blanket stitch. Ask a friend to help, and the job will go even faster.

## Let 'Em Weep!

If you have the common triple-track aluminum combination storm windows, make sure the weep holes aren't plugged. Those two little gaps at the bottom edge of the frame are designed to let rainwater drain from the sill. If the holes are blocked, your windows will not drain properly — and the wooden sill below will rot from moisture damage.

# HOW LONG HOUSEHOLD ITEMS LAST

The following life spans are merely a point of reference. Feel free to go for a longevity record! (Note: The life span of a product depends not only on its durability but also on your desire for some new convenience found only on a new model.)

| ITEM | YEARS *(approx. average)* |
|---|---|
| Electric shaver | 4 |
| Personal computer | 6 |
| Lawn mower | 6 |
| Automatic coffeemaker | 6 |
| VCR | 6 |
| Food processor | 7 |
| Electric can opener | 7 |
| CD player | 7 |
| Camcorder | 7 |
| Toaster | 8 |
| Stereo receiver | 8 |
| Color TV set | 8 |
| Blender | 8 |
| Room air conditioner | 9 |
| Vacuum cleaner | 10 |
| Microwave oven | 10 |
| Dishwasher | 11 |
| Dehumidifier | 12 |
| Washing machine | 13 |
| Electric dryer | 13 |
| Refrigerator | 14 |
| Gas dryer | 14 |
| Electric range | 15 |
| Gas range | 18 |

# OH, DARN!

Darning seems to have become a forgotten art. It's not hard to do, and it really prolongs the life of a garment. Don't throw out that wool sock with a hole in it! Stretch the sock over a darning egg, an orange, or a light bulb. Reinforce any frayed edges with running stitches (use thread) or trim the hole to a square. Find matching wool yarn and fill the hole with parallel running stitches. Next, weave across these lines at right angles until the hole is covered. Make sure you don't pull the stitches too tight. Weave the ends of the darning yarn back through the garment rather than making a bumpy knot. To mend a small item such as a thumb on a mitten, use a marble as a darning egg. Always match the color and weight of the mending yarn to the original article.

# HINTS & SUGGESTIONS

## Making Things Last

☞ For a quick, temporary fix, use melted wax to seal a small hole in a screen. Hold a dripping candle just above the hole and let the wax trickle down to fill in the breach.

☞ Press any leftover putty into the can. Cut a circle of wax paper and place it on top of the putty. Seal the can tightly, and it should remain usable for months. When you work with the putty again, moisten it with a few drops of linseed oil.

☞ To prepare paper logs for a cozy fire, roll old newspaper tightly into small logs, tie firmly, and soak in soapy water. Stand them on end to drain and dry.

☞ To cut down on sock darning, rub a little damp soap inside the heels and toes of clean socks and let dry. Repeat after washing.

☞ Do you have a bunch of mismatched but good nylons? Bring them to a boil in a pan of lightly salted water. Boil for a few minutes, then cool. They'll come out the same color.

> ∞○∞
>
> *O money, money, I am not necessarily*
> *one of those who thinks thee holy,*
> *But I often stop to wonder how thou*
> *canst go out so fast when thou*
> *comest in so slowly.*
>
> — OGDEN NASH (1902–1971)
>
> ∞○∞

# Getting to Know Your Dollar
# (Before You Give It Up)

*BY MRS. HENRY JOSEPHS*

Take a dollar bill and look closely at the back. Thereon you will see two circular imprints representing both sides of the Great Seal of the United States. Most of us are familiar with the figure of the American eagle clutching an olive branch in one talon and a brace of arrows in the other. However, few people can explain the mystical symbol in the left-hand circle, even though it appears on every one of the dollar bills now in circulation.

The founding fathers, desiring to express the basic truths on which the nation was established, incorporated them into the design of the Great Seal. On the afternoon the Declaration of Independence was signed, July 4, 1776, Thomas Jefferson, Benjamin Franklin, and John Adams were appointed as a committee to prepare the seal. Six years later, on June 20, 1782, Congress passed a resolution approving the final design.

According to William Barton, who

played an important part in creating the seal, the main part of the pyramid signifies the spiritual and material strength of the nation and its durability.

The eye in the radiant triangle above the pyramid is said to represent the eye of God. It also stresses the importance of putting the spiritual welfare of the country ahead of its material prosperity.

The words *Annuit Coeptis* above the symbol mean "He (God) has smiled on our undertakings." The eye and the motto also refer to the many noticeable interventions of Providence in favor of the American cause.

The three Latin words under the pyramid, *Novus Ordo Seclorum,* mean "A new order of the ages." They signify that the new republic introduced a new era in the lives and freedom of the people of the world — one in which the people themselves would be able to exercise their God-given rights to self-government.

The Roman numerals MDCCLXXVI at the base of the pyramid stand for 1776 — the beginning of the United States as an independent nation under God.

The dollar bill, besides being a medium of purchase throughout the land, also symbolizes the concept of the United States as a God-inspired nation.

# The Word *Dollar*

*Dollar* is a word that has passed through various forms: *thal, thaler, dahler, daalder, daler,* and *tallero.* It's originally from *Joachimstaler,* a coin made in Joachimsthal, Bohemia. This coin weighed one ounce and became so popular that it gave its name to the coins that came after it. The manufacture of this coin dates from about the year 1518.

# When to Dicker &
# When Not to Dicker          *BY PHILIP A. LINCOLN*

Old-time Yankees were noted for their sharp horse-trading. Their insistence on long, drawn-out dickering also extended to those who followed the sea. Consider Captain Colcord, master of the sailing vessel *Elizabeth* out of Belfast, Maine, bound from New York to San Francisco.

On February 21, 1891, reluctant to pay the usual $50 charge for being towed to the San Francisco Bay anchorage, Captain Colcord repeatedly turned down offers from several tugs to take him in tow. However, as his vessel proceeded under sail toward the anchorage, the weather worsened. Gusting winds and a strong ebb tide drove the *Elizabeth* relentlessly toward the rocky shoreline. One of the tug skippers, pointing out the increasing danger, again shouted that he would tow the *Elizabeth* safely to the anchorage for the standard $50.

Colcord offered him $25. The tug skipper refused. The wind was now approaching gale force with mounting seas. Colcord offered to split the difference.

"Make it $37.50!" he shouted.

Again the tug skipper refused. By this time, the *Elizabeth* had drifted dangerously close to shore. Unable now to control his vessel, Colcord grudgingly agreed to pay the $50, and the *Elizabeth* was taken in tow.

By now it was blowing a living gale. Suddenly, the tug's towing hawser parted, and the *Elizabeth* soon fetched up hard and fast on the rocky shore. Within 45 minutes, with her keel ripped off and her decks swept clean, she was reduced to a heaving mass of splintered planking and timbers. Of the 29 persons aboard, only 11 survived. Among them were the wife, son, and daughter of Captain Colcord. Eighteen were washed overboard and drowned, including the captain.

# I'm Frugal, You're Stingy

*Cheap* is one of those fuzzy philosophical concepts easily misapplied. Here are some standards you can use to gauge your thriftiness.

- ☞ **Frugal:** Drives 30 miles to save 25 cents on dishwashing detergent.

- ☞ **Stingy:** Makes $80,000 a year and allows unemployed friends to pick up the restaurant tab.

- ☞ **Sparing:** Reuses dental floss.

- ☞ **Economical:** Buys superduper-size jar of peanut butter. Uses rubber spatula to get last bit of peanut butter from jar.

- ☞ **Cheese-paring:** Watches public TV all year; never donates.

- ☞ **Parsimonious:** Gives free magazine subscription gift as wedding present.

- ☞ **Tightfisted:** Has a lot of money but shampoos own rugs.

- ☞ **Skinflint:** Tips 5 percent for *good* service.

# A Historical Incongrui-TEA?

**Question:** What I cannot understand is why a thrifty people like Yankees should have deliberately destroyed all that expensive tea at the Boston Tea Party. Do you know?

**Answer:** History merely states that they hove it overboard. Plenty of records show that coastal Yankees have always been very clever at salvaging goods from the sea.

# Living the Good Life
# on About 44 Cents a Day

According to a 1981 report from United Press International, Irene Prail of Dupo, Illinois, a 74-year-old widow, paid only $150 for food the previous year. "I've kept a record of everything I spent for food since 1975," she said. "I spent $127.29 in 1978 and about $35 more each year since. But I've had a good bit of company, and I haven't watched it as closely as I usually do."

Prail doesn't really need to pinch pennies but believes that most people spend far too much on food. "I don't drink milk, but I use canned evaporated milk on my cereal in the morning and for cooking," she said. "I never buy packaged things except for cake mixes. If I have company, I make my own rolls." She never buys soda, alcoholic beverages, cookies or other bakery goods, prepared goods such as pizzas, or paper products (except bath-

room tissue). Of course, she eats fresh vegetables from her backyard garden and cans or freezes the rest.

She favors chicken and other meats that sell for around a dollar a pound. She said that one chicken will last her several meals and a roast will last more than a week.

"Last night I had a breast of chicken and some doughnuts my neighbor gave me. She was going to throw them out. I sliced them in half, put a little butter in the bottom of my skillet, and warmed them up. They were delicious."

# SIX MONEY-SAVING TIPS
## (THAT YOU PROBABLY WON'T WANT TO TELL YOUR FRIENDS)

1. Whenever you see that someone has discarded a mop, broom, floor polisher, or other household item that has a wooden handle, stop and put it in your car. Cut off the worn-out portion and use the handle to tie up your tomatoes or support other plants in the garden. Use short wooden handles for rolling pins.

2. In winter, leave the water in the tub after you bathe until it reaches room temperature. Its heat and moisture will go into the room rather than down the drain.

3. Don't throw out your rolled-up tube of toothpaste. Instead, flatten it out, slice the tube with a razor blade, and scrape the remaining toothpaste with your brush. You'll get up to six more brushings from the tube.

4. When you cook spaghetti or macaroni, save the water. Let it sit for a few minutes, then skim the top and use the remaining liquid to starch your clothes and doilies.

5. When you open a new can of powdered cleanser, carefully scratch the adhesive covering from just one hole in the top, not all four. You'll find that you can shake out plenty of cleanser without using too much.

6. Cut steel wool soap pads in half before using; they'll go twice as far.

❦

*I have enough money to last me the rest of my life*
*— unless I buy something.*

— JACKIE MASON (b. 1931)

❦

# Burn Calories, Not Money

Keeping in shape can cost a lot of money unless you adopt a different (and more frugal) attitude toward the things you normally do. If you hustle through your chores to get to the fitness center, relax. You're getting a great workout already. The left-hand column below lists "chore" exercises, the middle column shows number of calories you burn per minute per pound of body weight, and the right-hand column lists comparable "recreational" exercises (if no number is given in parentheses, it's the same as for the chore). For example, a 150-pound person forking straw bales burns 9.45 calories per minute, the same workout he or she would get playing basketball.

| | | |
|---|---|---|
| Ax chopping, fast | 0.135 | Skiing, cross-country — uphill (0.125) |
| Climbing hills, with 44-pound load | 0.066 | Swimming, crawl — fast (0.071) |
| Digging trenches | 0.065 | Skiing, cross-country — steady walk |
| Forking straw bales | 0.063 | Basketball |
| Chopping down trees | 0.060 | Football |
| Climbing hills, with 9-pound load | 0.058 | Swimming, crawl — slow |
| Sawing by hand | 0.055 | Skiing, cross-country — moderate |
| Lawn mowing | 0.051 | Horseback riding, trotting (0.050) |
| Scrubbing floors | 0.049 | Tennis |
| Shoveling coal | 0.049 | Aerobic dance, medium |
| Hoeing | 0.041 | Weight training, circuit training (0.042) |
| Stacking firewood | 0.040 | Weightlifting, free weights (0.039) |
| Shoveling grain | 0.038 | Golf |
| House painting | 0.035 | Walking, normal pace — asphalt road |
| Weeding | 0.033 | Table tennis (0.031) |
| Food shopping | 0.028 | Cycling, 5.5 mph (0.029) |
| Mopping floors | 0.028 | Fishing |
| Window cleaning | 0.026 | Croquet |
| Raking | 0.025 | Dancing, ballroom (0.023) |
| Driving a tractor | 0.016 | Drawing, in standing position |

# Bread Made of Wood

*We leave you with this last example of economy — an extreme measure of resourcefulness, to be sure, but proof that one really can get along without the luxuries. It comes from* The Emigrant's Handbook *(1854). We sincerely hope that you will never be faced with such a challenge.*

"In times of great scarcity, and where famine threatens, it is well known how to prepare a nutritious substance, which may go under the name of bread, from the beech and other woods destitute of turpentine.

"Take green wood, chop it into very small chips; or make it into shavings, which is better. Boil these three or four times, stirring them very hard during boiling. Dry them, and then reduce them to powder, if possible; if not, as fine as you can. Bake this powder in the oven three or four times, and then grind it as you would corn. Wood thus prepared acquires the smell and taste of corn flour. It will not ferment without the addition of leaven. The leaven prepared for corn-flour is the best to use with it.

"It will form a spongy bread, and when much baked with a hard crust, is by no means unpalatable.

"This kind of flour, boiled in water and left to stand, forms a thick, tough, trembling jelly, which is very nutritious, and in time of great scarcity in frontier countries, may be restored to preserve life, with perfect confidence."

# Text Credits

## Chapter 1

pp. 19–23, "Paper Clutter": From "Getting Rid of Paper Clutter," *The Old Farmer's Almanac*, 1996.

p. 24, "What to Do with the Stuff You Usually Throw Away": From *The Old Farmer's Almanac*, 1984.

pp. 25–30, "Dry & Cool, or How to Keep Things Fresh": From "Ways to Store Everything," *The Old Farmer's Almanac*, 1996.

p. 31, "In Praise of the Pantry": From *The Old Farmer's Almanac Hearth & Home Calendar*, 1996.

## Chapter 2

p. 38, "When to Call In the Pros": From *The Practical Guide to Practically Everything* edited by Peter Bernstein & Christopher Ma. N.Y.: Random House, 1995.

pp. 39–41, "How Long Is a Furrow?": From *The Old Farmer's Almanac*, 1972.

p. 42, "Origins of Old-Time (Premetric) Measuring Units": From *The Old Farmer's Almanac*, 1983.

p. 42, "Makeshift Measurers": From *The Old Farmer's Almanac Special Reference Edition*, 1997.

p. 43, "Metric Conversion": From *The Old Farmer's Almanac Special Reference Edition*, 1997.

p. 44, "Homeowner's Tool Kit": From *The*

*Old Farmer's Almanac Special Reference Edition*, 1997.

pp. 45–48, "Up Against the Wallpaper": From *The Old Farmer's Almanac Home-Owner's Companion*, 1996.

pp. 49–51, "Painting Pointers": From "Wondering What Color to Paint It? The *Old Farmer's Almanac HomeOwner's Companion*, 1996.

p. 50, "Working With the Weather": From *The Old Farmer's Almanac HomeOwner's Companion*, 1996.

p. 52, "Tricks for Painters": From Check Out the Cupboard, Not the Hardware Store," *The Old Farmer's Almanac HomeOwner's Companion*, 1996.

## Chapter 3

pp. 61–63, "How to Avoid a Draining Experience" and "Signs of Big Backups": From *The Old Farmer's Almanac HomeOwner's Companion*, 1996.

p. 64, "Necessary Business": From "A Look Back: Plumbing and Sanitation in the Good(?) Old Days," *The Old Farmer's Almanac*, 1989.

p. 65, "Something to Think About": From *The Old Farmer's Almanac*, 1982.

p. 65, "How Much Water Does a Steak Dinner Cost?": *From The Old Farmer's Almanac*, 1983.

p. 66, "How Much Water is Used?": From

*The Old Farmer's Almanac Special Reference Edition*, 1997.

pp. 67–70, "The Once and Future Fuse Box": From *The Old Farmer's Almanac HomeOwner's Companion*, 1995.

p. 71, "How Much Electricity is Used?": From *The Old Farmer's Almanac Special Reference Edition*, 1997.

p. 72, "Check Your Light Bulbs in Fall": From *The Old Farmer's Almanac*, 1939.

## Chapter 4

pp. 79–89, "The Virtues of Vinegar, Lemons & Salt": From "Everything You Never Thought You Could Do with Vinegar" by Earl W. Proulx, *The Old Farmer's Almanac*, 1989; "Unexpected Uses for Soap and Suds" by Raymond Schuessler, *The Old Farmer's Almanac*, 1984; "The Miracle of the Common Everyday Lemon," *The Old Farmer's Almanac*, 1980; "Herbs That Can Help Around the House" by Barbara Radcliffe Rogers, *The Old Farmer's Almanac*, 1979; "Salt: It's Still Worth It's Salt" by Fran White, *The Old Farmer's Almanac*, 1992; "Salt: Your Spartan Servant," *The Old Farmer's Almanac*, 1974; "Check Out the Cupboard, Not the Hardware Store," *The Old Farmer's Almanac HomeOwner's Companion*, 1996.

pp. 80, 85, 92, "Working With the Weather": From *The Old Farmer's Almanac HomeOwner's Companion*, 1996.

pp. 90–91, "From Carpet Beaters to Suction Sweepers": From "Buyers Beware," *The Old Farmer's Almanac Hearth & Home Companion*, 1994.

p. 91, "Where Does Dust Come From?": From "Where Does Dirt Come From," *The Old Farmer's Almanac Hearth & Home Companion*, 1994.

p. 92, "An Old Epitaph to Ponder": From *The Old Farmer's Almanac*, 1980.

## Chapter 5

p. 100, "Tugging at the Heart of It": From *The Book of Love* by Christine Schultz, copyright © by Yankee Publishing Inc. Published by Villard Books.

p. 101, "Rearing Young Children": From "Hints on the Rearing of Young Children of

Two to Three Years," *The Old Farmer's Almanac*, 1937.

pp. 102–103, "Good Old Games": From "Games People Used to Play," *The Old Farmer's Almanac*, 1972.

pp. 104–105, "Family Medicine Chest": From *The Old Farmer's Almanac*, 1939, and *The Old Farmer's Almanac Special Reference Edition*, 1997.

p. 105, "Emergency Car Kit": From *The Old Farmer's Almanac Special Reference Edition*, 1997.

pp. 107–110, "Eight Rules for Pet Owners": From "the Worst Mistakes Animal Lovers Make," *The Old Farmer's Almanac Hearth & Home Companion*, 1994.

p. 110, "Doggy Demeanor": From *The Old Farmer's Almanac Special Reference Edition*, 1997.

p. 111, "Why Do Cats Eat Grass?": From *The Old Farmer's Almanac*, 1988.

p. 111, "Don't Poison Your Pussycat": From *The Old Farmer's Almanac Special Reference Edition*, 1997.

p. 112, "Carpet CAT-astrophe!": From "When Your Pet Makes a Wet Boo-boo on the Carpet," *The Old Farmer's Almanac*, 1985.

## Chapter 6

p. 119, "Carpenter Ants and Termites": From *Earl Proulx's Yankee Home Hints* by Earl Proulx and the Editors of Yankee Magazine. Published by Yankee Books, a division of Yankee Publishing, Inc., 1993.

pp. 120–122, "The Cockroach, or A Lesson in Survival": From *The Old Farmer's Almanac HomeOwner's Companion*, 1995.

p. 123, "The Cricket on Your Hearth": From "Where Creatures ARE Stirring," *The Old Farmer's Almanac Hearth & Home Companion*, 1994.

pp. 124–125, "Homespun Remedies for Fleas"and "A Few Facts About the Infamous Flea": From *The Old Farmer's Almanac*, 1990.

pp. 126–127, "A Fly in Your Buttermilk?": From *The Old Farmer's Almanac HomeOwner's Companion*, 1996.

p. 128, "The Prolific Housefly": From "How

Many Descendants Can a Mother Housefly Produce in Six Months?" *The Old Farmer's Almanac*, 1978.

p. 129, "The Battle of the Moths": From *The Old Farmer's Almanac*, 1935.

p. 130, "The House Mouse": From "Where Creatures ARE Stirring," *The Old Farmer's Almanac Hearth & Home Companion*, 1994.

p. 131, "Rat Control": From *The Old Farmer's Almanac*, 1951.

p. 131, "An Antisquirrel Hint": From *The Old Farmer's Almanac*, 1980.

### Chapter 7

p. 139, "First Aid for Furniture": From "Some Good Ways to Repair Wooden Furniture," *The Old Farmer's Almanac*, 1981.

pp. 140–141, "Where Would We Be Without Duct Tape?": From *The Old Farmer's Almanac Hearth & Home Companion*, 1995.

p. 142, "Window Wisdom": From "Mending Screens," *The Old Farmer's Almanac Hearth & Home Calendar*, 1997; "Weeping is Good For Them" *Yankee Magazine's Make It Last* by Earl Proulx and the Editors of Yankee Magazine. Yankee Books, a division of Yankee Publishing, Inc., 1996.

p. 143, "How Long Household Items Last": From *The Old Farmer's Almanac Special Reference Edition*, 1997.

p. 144, "Oh, Darn!": From *The Old Farmer's Almanac Hearth & Home Calendar*, 1997.

pp. 145–146, "Getting to Know Your Dollar": From "Becoming Better Acquainted with Your Money (Before You Give It Up)," *The Old Farmer's Almanac*, 1974.

**p. 146, "The Word Dollar": From *The Old Farmer's Almanac*, 1957.

p. 147, "When to Dicker and When Not to Dicker": From *The Old Farmer's Almanac*, 1984.

p. 148, "I'm Frugal, You're Stingy": From "The New England Sampler," *Yankee Magazine*, September 1991.

**p. 148, "A Historical Incongrui-TEA?": From *Weatherwise & Otherwise* by Joseph Chase Allen. Yankee, Inc., 1974.

p. 149, "Living the Good Life on About 44 Cents a Day": From *The Old Farmer's Almanac*, 1981.

p. 150, "Six Money-Saving Tips": From *The Old Farmer's Almanac Hearth & Home Companion*, 1995.

p. 151, "Burn Calories, Not Money": From "Calorie Burning," *The Old Farmer's Almanac Special Reference Edition*, 1997.

p. 152, "Bread Made of Wood": From *The Old Farmer's Almanac*, 1973.

# Index